ÎLE DE FRANCE AND LIBERTÉ

Festive occasion! *Liberté* departs from New York's Pier 88 on 24 May 1952. The caption read: 'Full load – 1,425 passengers onboard'. (Cronican-Arroyo Collection)

ÎLE DE FRANCE AND LIBERTÉ

FRANCE'S PREMIER POST-WAR LINERS

WILLIAM H. MILLER

The
History
Press

First published 2013

The History Press
The Mill, Brimscombe Port
Stroud, Gloucestershire, GL5 2QG
www.thehistorypress.co.uk

British Library Cataloguing in Publication Data.
A catalogue record for this book is available from the British Library.

ISBN 978 0 7524 7486 1

Typesetting and origination by The History Press
Printed in Turkey

CONTENTS

Foreword   7

Acknowledgements   8

Introduction   9

1 Preface to *Île de France* and *Liberté*   11

2 Pre-War Veteran: *De Grasse* (1924)   13

3 The Splendid *Île de France*   14

4 Flagship of the Fleet: *Liberté*   37

5 To the West Indies: *Colombie*   84

6 French Twins: *Flandre* & *Antilles*   86

7 Cruising French Style: the *De Grasse* of 1956   88

8 Other Liners Under the Tricolour   89

9 Replacement & the Future: *France*   92

Bibliography   96

FOREWORD

It was May 1953 and the family was off for the great adventure. Mother had emigrated from Denmark twenty-two years earlier and father thought it time to make the big trip back to her homeland and meet the family. As a child, little did I comprehend the distances we were about to embark upon. It was a time when travel to Europe was something very uncommon for the average American family. One needed not only money, but a considerable amount of time, including mental and physical endurance for such a trip. Europe was a long way from southern California.

I am not sure that my father had in mind any specific ocean liner when he made our travel arrangements at Downey Travel; in fact, I rather doubt he did. But I owe my love of the SS *Île de France* today to the arrangements made that day. On both the eastbound and return trip it was our good fortune to be on board this beautiful and honourable ocean liner. Little did I know at the time that she was one of the most beloved of ocean liners of all time.

After travelling a week in the family's Nash Ambassador some 3,000 miles across the country, we finally arrived in New York City, the likes of which I had never before seen. Naturally, I was initially overwhelmed with the size of the buildings, but then we soon embarked on the biggest 'boat' I had ever seen in my short life. It was so big that our car was being lifted into its belly. She was a beautiful ship, a most marvellous sight sitting there berthed at Pier 88, as if she was waiting just for my family. Once on board, I was struck by the unique nature of its interiors and all the beautiful wood panelling found almost everywhere. I did not know how to describe it then; I did not really understand what the decor meant, but I knew it had

a special and unique feeling about it – one I would not experience again until I walked on to the *Queen Mary* in Long Beach years later. Of course, the originality of Art Deco that was the *Île* was not understood by me at the time. As a child, I quickly associated that feel and that look with big ocean liners. I did not realise that the SS *United States* just a pier over from us was so radically different. But for me to this day, Art Deco equates to ocean liners.

Today, I feel privileged to have experienced the *Île de France*, the wonderful service that the French were so well known for on their liners, whether it was in the dining rooms, up on the sun deck or in the staterooms. It seemed that no matter where we were on the ship, the stewards would find us just to provide refreshments and service of all sorts. Of course, what I remember the most was the wafers and ice cream. I found myself becoming very comfortable and content as a child even though I was so far from home. And then there was the children's playroom, with its hobby horses, the Punch & Judy puppet shows in the corner and all the fun craft projects, that was made available for the kids.

Finally, I strongly remember having to leave my newly found 'home', this beautiful liner, and disembarking so early on that cold June morning on to the tender in the middle of the bay in Plymouth, England. Travel to visit family in Europe was quite the adventure in those wonderful days. In many ways, I miss it so.

Allen Pellymounter
Chula Vista, California

ACKNOWLEDGEMENTS

It is much like the crew of the *Île de France* and *Liberté*: it takes many hands to operate a ship and, comparatively, many to assemble a book. There are the illustrations, the covers and the anecdotes, reflections and recollections to be gathered, assembled and organised into a fitting tribute, in this case to two fine liners. First, my great thanks to The History Press for taking on this project and especially to Amy Rigg and Abigail Wood. They've done a superb job in the book's final production.

Then, also at the very top of the list, are sharing, generous friends: Philippe Brebant, Richard Faber, Norman Knebel, Anton Logvinenko (for the colourisation of the cover) and to Allen Pellymounter (for his thoughtful and evocative Foreword). Other kind supporters and contributors include: Ernest Arroyo, the late Werner Bamberger, Naomi Jolles Barry, Luis Miguel Correia, the late Lewis and Ruth Gordon, the late Alex Duncan, Peter Fialkowski, Brian Hawley, Andy Hernandez, the late George Horne, June Jones, Hisashi Noma, Fred Rodriguez, Reverend Neville Rucker, Don Stoltenberg, Jane Bouche Strong and the late Horace Sutton.

Companies and organisations that have further assisted include: Compagnie Generale Transatlantique (the French Line), Halifax Maritime Museum, Hapag-Lloyd, Moran Towing & Transportation Company, Norwegian Cruise Lines, Photofest and the Port Authority of New York & New Jersey.

INTRODUCTION

Great, oversized and, most of all, richly colourful advertisements, usually spread across the pages of glossy magazines, were often suggestive, even fanciful, certainly evocative. Myself, I've collected many of them, often carefully extracted from the pages of long-ago *Holiday* and *National Geographic*. One of them – and one of my top favourites – is a night-time view of the aft, open decks of a great ocean liner bound for Europe. Passengers are sketched in fine, colourful fashions, standing, chatting, but mostly dancing and all under the stars. Then there are the lit-up ship's windows and portholes. Yellowed stars fill the sky above while the seawater surrounding the ship is inky blue. But perhaps most evocative are the lighted funnels, the ship's characteristic smokestacks. In this case, they are mostly tomato red, but with charcoal black tops. These were the colours of the great French Line, a company name actually used mostly outside French borders. It was the CGT or 'Transat' – Compagnie Generale Transatlantique – to the French themselves. They were all but 'blessed' with the most glorious identity, the grandest of reputations and the most romantic imagery. Their sailings on the Atlantic, to and from the French port of Le Havre, were dubbed (and aptly so) as 'France afloat'. In itself, it hinted at the flawless food and dining, the impeccable service; indeed, at the gayest and most romantic liners on the Atlantic.

Following the huge disruption of the Second World War, transatlantic ocean liner services were gradually revived and then boomed, especially in the 1950s. Everyone, so it seemed, was travelling again. In lavish, luxuriant first class, there were the film stars, business tycoons and even royalty. Along with them came personal servants, dogs in the ship's kennels and glittering jewels safely stored in the purser's safe. Great, gleaming American cars were stowed in the holds and readied for European touring. And, of course, there were those bulky trunks – usually the big cocoa-coloured creations by Vuitton – on board the French liners. In less expensive cabins and even cheaper tourist-class quarters were the legions of camera-toting tourists, the students and the teachers, and the last wave of, say, French immigrants bound for America. There were shared cabins, summer attire for those two- and three-week guided tours (and in that age of 'Europe-on-$5-a day'), well-read guide books and then maybe, just maybe, the chance of a shipboard romance. In the holds, even of great liners, were the prized, high-quality cargoes: the mail, automobiles, gold bullion and, rather expectedly on French ships, loads of the latest Paris fashions. Chanel and Dior couture creations were almost always on the cargo manifests.

By the war's end in the summer of 1945, however, the great, Paris-headquartered French Line was almost in ruins. All but two of their pre-war liners were gone. Even the exquisite *Normandie*, an 83,000-tonner, 2,000-passenger ship that had been appraised by many as the most luxurious Atlantic liner ever built, was gone. She had burned at New York – in fact, at the French Line's terminal, at Pier 88, along the City's West Side, in February 1942. She then capsized, had to be partially scrapped before being salvaged, righted and, with war's end, the $60 million ship of 'genius & beauty' was sold to local scrappers. Her remains fetched a mere $161,000. Otherwise, noted pre-war liners such as the *Paris*, *Lafayette* and *Champlain* were gone as well. By 1946, the much-reduced French Line was forced to restore their primary service to New York with nothing more than two converted freighters – the *Oregon* and the *Wisconsin* – each carrying a mere seventy-five passengers. Expectedly, as passenger traffic and even European tourism resumed, every sailing was booked to capacity.

However, happier, more luxurious and certainly more glorious days were ahead. By the 1950s, the French had two of the very finest liners in the world handling their transatlantic schedules. The *Île de France*, a ship of the most extraordinary reputation, based mostly on her innovative decor and superlative kitchens, from her pre-war days (she was commissioned in 1927), was restored by 1949 and to some she was better than ever. She was like, one frequent passenger told me, a 'middle-aged lady that was cosmetically invigorated with two instead of her original three funnels'. She looked handsome, to others absolutely *magnifique*! Her interiors were as decoratively splendid as ever – from the Lalique chandeliers and Aubusson carpets to the finest woods and best French crystal. But if her reputation again had a peak, it was for her cooking. She was said to be the best-fed liner on the Atlantic. Yes, her earlier reputation was intact: more seagulls followed the *Île de France* than any other ship!

France also needed a grand national flagship, to replace the sumptuous *Normandie*, and through post-war reparations in 1946 was given the German superliner *Europa*. She too was cosmetically overhauled and enhanced and, rather expectedly, 'de-Germanised'. Proudly flying the Tricolour and capped by twin funnels in that classic red and black, she was recommissioned in the summer of 1950 as the *Liberté*. With sumptuous accommodations and exquisite menus, she soon amassed the most enviable reputation.

To sail aboard *Île de France* and *Liberté* was said to be the 'cheeriest way' to cross the Atlantic. In tribute and recollection, this book is about their life and times: the ships themselves, their innards and, of course, those who sailed them. They were, without question, 'France afloat'. We also look, if briefly, at other French Line passenger ships of the period: the restored, pre-war *De Grasse*, the *Colombie* on the colonial West Indies route and, again like Parisian fashions, the 'new creations' of the early 1950s, the near-sisters *Flandre* and *Antilles*. There's also a glance, if you will, at other French passenger ship services: the French Line itself to North Africa, and then firms such as Messageries Maritimes, Compagnie de Sud-Atlantique, Chargeurs Reunis, Compagnie Mixte and others. They created, as if in a French play, the 'supporting cast' to *Île de France* and *Liberté*. Of course, both of those big liners needed replacement by the late 1950s and so we will look as well at their combined replacement: the magnificent *France*, completed in 1962.

An advertising poster of the day seemed to say it all about the French Line, their style and their ships. It showed a tall, beautiful glass, elegant and crafted, filled with fine champagne. Bubbles, a collection of them, emerged, hinting at the joy of shipboard living and the great, grand days of two of the world's finest, most popular and certainly immensely interesting ocean liners, *Île de France* and *Liberté*.

Bill Miller
Secaucus, New Jersey

1

PREFACE TO *ÎLE DE FRANCE* AND *LIBERTÉ*

In the summer of 1945, with the war in Europe finally over, the French Line, like so many others, was anxious to resume its passenger service, especially the one connecting with America. But there were no available passenger ships for them, at least at the time. The great *Île de France* was still trooping and, after enormous refitting, would not actually return to commercial service until the summer of 1949. The smaller *De Grasse* was just being salvaged, following her deliberate sinking by the vengeful Nazis, but she too needed extensive repairs and upgrading. She would not return to service until the spring of 1947. Otherwise, the legendary French Line ships such as the *Paris*, *Lafayette*, *Champlain* and, worst of all, the *Normandie* were gone. With a pressing demand for transatlantic passages, Paris officials decided instead to take the twenty-eight-passenger freighter *Wisconsin* and triple her quarters to seventy-six, all one class, by adding bunks to each cabin. She was used on the run between Le Havre and Manhattan's Pier 88. She was an interim ship, of course; a mere 7,000-tonner that was not only slow but aged, yet run as close to French Line standards as possible.

'We started our "love affair" with the Transat [Compagnie Generale Transatlantique] in 1948. We took a no-frills, one-class ship called the *Wisconsin*,' recalled Jane Bouche Strong, a one-time editor of *Gourmet* magazine in New York City:

The spirits that were left from our Pier 88 bon voyage party with family and friends were carted aboard to fuel parties with new found friends during the journey. When all that remained was a half bottle of Chilean wine, we took it to the barman (in what was only a service bar; there were no public rooms as such on this vessel), who, upon uncorking it, cried, 'You don't want this!' and promptly poured it out the porthole.

Classic ocean liner! The three-funnel *Paris*, the prelude to the *Île de France*, departs from New York with the Brooklyn shoreline in the background. (Cronican-Arroyo Collection)

Each meal was taken by all passengers at a single sitting: lunch at 11:45, dinner at 7. There was no choice in the food, but everything served was excellent. In eleven days, we never had potatoes prepared in the same way twice, and I learned not to be repelled by fish served with the head.

The smaller, single-funnel *Champlain* prepares to set off on her maiden voyage in June 1932. She was a prelude to the brilliant *Normandie*. (Cronican-Arroyo Collection)

The exquisite *Normandie* departs from New York in October 1938 but with only 150 passengers aboard because of the threat of war in Europe. (French Line)

Ocean liner style: film queen Marlene Dietrich sails from New York with thirty-eight pieces of luggage aboard the *Normandie* in 1937. (Photofest)

Mrs Strong concluded:

As plain as all this, the famed *atmosphere Transat* was evident. The crew was solicitous and witty, and, if you spoke French, there were cozy little parties in the officers' quarters. In the absence of salons, we danced on the narrow deck to the current songs of Piaf, Trenet and Montand played on a Victrola. Upon arrival at Le Havre, we were saddened to see that almost all the buildings had been flattened in the war, but the sight of the crew's families lined up along the jetty, waving to welcome them home, restored our spirits.

Three wartime liners from another French passenger ship company, Messageries Maritimes – the *Marechal Joffre*, *Indochinois* and *Athos II* – assisted on an austere, very temporary French Line passenger service to New York in 1945–46. Normally on the Le Havre–Caribbean run, the *Colombie*, which belonged to the French Line, made a few austerity crossings as well.

2

PRE-WAR VETERAN: *DE GRASSE* (1924)

Having been built in 1924 for New York sailings as well as Le Havre–Caribbean service and cruising, the 17,707grt *De Grasse* was a secondary, intermediate passenger ship for the French. She'd been deliberately scuttled by the Nazis in their retreat on 30 August 1944. It took a year to refloat the 574ft-long vessel and then a further two years to restore her at St Nazaire. She resumed luxury service in the summer of 1947 and first appeared in New York on 25 July. 'The *De Grasse* was the prelude to the *Île de France* and *Liberté*,' remembered Lewis Gordon. 'A pleasant ship and certainly filling an important role [between 1947 and 1949], she was by no means as luxurious as the two larger liners.' In 1952, the 970-passenger ship was moved permanently to

West Indies service, but then was sold, quite suddenly, to Canadian Pacific Steamships.

Philippe Brebant, an ocean liner historian and journalist living in Le Havre, noted:

Although older and ageing, the *De Grasse* most likely would have been retained for several more years by the French Line. But Canadian Pacific needed a passenger ship urgently [in January 1953] after their *Empress of Canada* had burned and then capsized at Liverpool. With the Coronation of Queen Elizabeth II coming that June, Canadian Pacific was expecting record numbers of ships and so could not be short of berths. They offered extra monies to the French for the *De Grasse*, which was bought and then quickly became the *Empress of Australia*.

Sold again in 1956, the ex-*De Grasse* now became the *Venezuela* for Italy's Grimaldi-Siosa Lines. She was stranded on the rocks near Cannes in March 1962, became a complete loss and was later scrapped.

6lo7 Venezuela   1924 18.567 Sicula Oceanica ex"De Grasse"

The ex-*De Grasse* of 1924 in her final career as the Italian *Venezuela*. (Author's Collection)

3

THE SPLENDID *ÎLE DE FRANCE*

The *Île de France* was the first large liner to be designed and built after the First World War. At the time of her construction, the headquarters in Paris of the French Line were already and enthusiastically predicting that she would be the most magnificent liner on the Atlantic. She was not, however, intended to be the biggest or fastest liner of her day. In fact, she had no statistical notations other than being the largest French liner to date and, of course, the flagship of the French merchant marine. Her outer appearance was rather ordinary. It was simply modelled on numerous other liners: three evenly slanted funnels with two large masts. But the French Line's exuberant excitement was ignited by her interiors, which were quite simply revolutionary, innovative, even startling. She was boldly, perhaps brazenly modern. Nothing like her had been seen before. Like those new fashions from Paris, she was an individual, not following designs and styles seen before. She was a trendsetter, an innovator, the 'inventor' of the new 'ocean liner style'. She initiated and introduced the moderne in shipboard decor that would lead to the hugely popular Art Deco on the high seas. Fleets of other liners would follow in her wake and culminate, by 1935, with another exquisite French liner, the extraordinary *Normandie*. *Île de France* had the sensational style that ocean liner collector and historian Stephen Lash would later dub 'early Ginger Rogers'. Hollywood would, like the designers of skyscrapers, hotels, railway stations and department stores, copy and enhance the style first seen two years before the *Île* was commissioned, in 1925, at the Exposition of Decorative Arts in Paris. The designers of the ship had, it was accurately reported, created the first true luxury floating resort. And in the words of French Line president Piaz, 'To live is not to copy'.

The construction of the 791ft-long *Île de France* was underwritten by the French Government as part of an agreement with the French Line, the Compagnie Generale Transatlantique, that dated from 1912. In the wake of the completion of the four-funnel, 23,666grt *France*, the pact called for the construction of four passenger liners in five-year intervals: 1916, 1921, 1926 and 1931. The 34,569grt *Paris* was laid down in 1914 to fulfil the 1916 category, but the First World War greatly disrupted her construction such that the 764ft-long ship was not completed until 1921. Consequently, the second ship, *Île de France*, was rescheduled from 1921 to 1926–27.

On 11 March 1926, at the Penhoet Shipyards of St Nazaire and amidst the presence of thousands of French Government officials, French Line directors and managers, workers, their families and many other invited guests, this second ship was formally named *Île de France* (Isle of France) and launched into the River Loire. Fourteen months later, on 29 May 1927, the 43,153grt ship left the shipyard for her first sea trials, which were pleasing and resulted in a 23½-knot top speed. She then returned for a brief survey and to fine-tune adjustments at Brest before proceeding

Hollywood stars seemed to favour the French Line and its ships. Here Errol Flynn signs autographs for the bell boys aboard the *Île de France* in 1934. (Photofest)

Splendour at sea! The outbound *Île de France* dressed in flags for her maiden crossing to New York in June 1927. (Andreas Hernandez Collection)

A French threesome! From left to right, *Île de France*, *France* and *Paris* berthed together at Le Havre. (Richard Faber Collection)

LE HAVRE. - PORT AUTONOME. - Les Paquebots " Ile de-France ", " France " et " Paris "
au Quai Joann's-Couvert

Novelty on the high seas! In July 1928, a catapult was fitted to the stern section of *Île de France*. Within weeks, and for the first time on a commercial ship, a mail-carrying seaplane was launched 500 miles off New York, where it arrived at French Line's Pier 57, at the foot of West 15th Street. The plane took three hours and cut a full day off the usual delivery time. (Luis Miguel Correia Collection)

to Le Havre, her home port, where she berthed on 5 June. Soon, she was opened for public inspection and tours. Tens of thousands toured her innards, but it was the press that was all but wildly enthusiastic and top heavy with praise of the luxuries and novelties displayed in the sparkling *Île de France*.

The first-class staterooms, which altogether numbered 390, were done in many different styles and led one writer to say: 'The *Île* is more eclectic than modern.' Overall, she heralded what would become the Art Deco age on the high seas with her simplified, angular furniture, sweeping and tall columns, inventive as well as creative lighting and an overall but very evident sense of spaciousness. Each public room, it seemed, was unique. The first-class bar was said to be the longest afloat, a distinction much appreciated by thirsty Americans then caught in the bite of national Prohibition. The main restaurant in first class, again noted as the largest of its kind yet to go to sea, rose three decks in height and had a spectacular staircase as a main entrance. First-class ladies especially, from Hollywood stars to New York socialites to European royals, absolutely loved this space, it was widely reported, for the effect of dazzling entrances. The grand foyer was even higher, with four decks, and the Gothic-styled chapel

had fourteen pillars and Stations of the Cross. Special amenities included a shooting gallery, a merry-go-round for children and a well-equipped gymnasium.

Accommodation was arranged for 1,586 passengers in all: 670 in first class, 408 in cabin class and 508 in third class. All cabins, including those in third class, had the novelty of having beds instead of bunks. First class contained a large assortment of suites and deluxe staterooms, and was soon dubbed the finest selection of high-end quarters on the Atlantic. Within eight years, by 1935, *Île de France* had carried more first-class passengers than any other transatlantic liner.

On 22 June 1927, she sailed from Le Havre to a rousing send-off. After a brief call at Plymouth, she crossed the Atlantic in six days; she reached New York and received a joyous reception. She berthed at Pier 57, French Line's terminal at the foot of West 15th Street in Manhattan's Chelsea section. Amidst the family of great Atlantic liners, the steam-turbine, quadruple-screw *Île* was an immediate success. Within her first decade, she was one of the ten most popular liners on the Atlantic, averaging 795 passengers per crossing, and this included the deep months of winter, even in the sluggish, all-but-devastating early Depression years.

The exquisite grand dining salon, then the largest of its kind afloat, as photographed in September 1933. (French Line)

85 — LE PAQUEBOT « ILE DE FRANCE », de la Compagnie Générale Transatlantique. Une Cheminée — LL

A workman attends to the whistles attached to the forward funnel aboard *Île de France*. (French Line)

The first-class grand salon aboard *Île de France* in a view also dated 1933. (French Line)

Almost from the start she developed an immense reputation coupled with her great popularity. It was said that she had an on-board style, an ambience that was unlike any other liner, even the other French liners. The *Île* was described as 'the cheeriest way to cross the Atlantic' and, with such definitive style, as a 'bit of mainland France herself'. Himself a seasoned traveller as well as ocean liner historian and collector, the late Everett Viez once said: 'In the 1930s, it was said that for the very best time when crossing the Atlantic, there was without any doubt only one ship – the *Île de France*!'

The *Île*, it seems, had one blemish. She suffered from noticeable, often serious vibrations. In 1933, she was sent back to her builders at St Nazaire, where every piece of wood panelling was removed, padded and then reinserted. While there, the *Île* sat not far from *Normandie*, the greatest and grandest of all French liners. While still unnamed at the time, that 1,028ft-long ship was dubbed 'the super-*Île de France*'. She was a direct descendant of the *Île*, but even more innovative, revolutionary, glamorous and stunning. Like the *Île* herself, the *Normandie* would be one of the most outstanding ocean liners ever to sail the Atlantic in the twentieth century.

As war in Europe dramatically and cruelly erupted on 3 September 1939, the *Île* was in safe waters, moored on the south side of Pier 88, just across the rooftop from *Normandie*. Such celebrated Atlantic queens as *Queen Mary*, *Aquitania* and *Conte di Savoia* were also nearby. As with the giant *Normandie*, the French Government in Paris was unwilling to have some ships make risky returns to their homeland. But soon the *Île* was occupying a much-needed berth and so, within two months, in November, a small armada of 10 Moran Towing Company tugs moved the otherwise 'dead ship' down the Hudson and across the Upper and Lower Bays to a berth on Staten Island. She sat there lifeless, unlit by night, soon repainted in sombre wartime grey and had her caretaker staff drastically reduced from 800 to 100. But as the war in Europe escalated, France was at greater risk of invasion by the Nazis and the need to use large liners as high-capacity troopships was becoming increasingly urgent; the *Île* was placed, as of 1 March 1940, on loan to the British Admiralty. In April she was prepared for sea duties and, on 1 May, set sail from Staten Island. While her final destination was top secret, she was loaded with 2,400 tons of war materiel, had barrels of oil in her holds and had three airplanes secured to her aft and outer deck (and a few others below). Three passengers were aboard as well. Eventually, the ship found her way to the distant waters of Singapore.

The grey-painted, already hard-worked *Île* did not return to New York for another year and a half, until the autumn of 1941. Handed over to

War clouds in Europe are forming. *Île de France* sets off from Le Havre in this view dated 1939. (Richard Faber Collection)

Uncertainty at New York as four liners wait in limbo – *Île de France* is on the far left, at Pier 88; next to her is *Normandie*, *Queen Mary* and *Aquitania*. On the far right is *Rex*, still sailing for Mussolini's Italy in service to and from the Mediterranean. (Cronican-Arroyo Collection)

Heavily loaded with returning troops, *Île de France*, under Cunard-White Star management, arrives at Halifax in this view from 1945. (Halifax Maritime Museum)

Waiting for orders at a Staten Island pier off New York's Lower Bay, *Île de France* is being prepared for war service in this photograph dated 28 April 1940. (Gillespie-Faber Collection)

the local Todd Shipyards in Brooklyn, she was given a thorough 120-day conversion for increased and further trooping. Shipyard crews worked round the clock. In the end, there was official berthing for 9,706 military passengers, new kitchen facilities, a full refit for her propulsion systems and the scrapping and replacement of her entire plumbing system. Soon she was returned to the British, under P&O Line's management, for trooping in and around the Far East. With French officers, she was now manned largely by an Asiatic crew, which included Indian Lascars so familiar to P&O operations. Serving the Allies, she sailed under dual flags: Britain and Free France.

The *Île* was at first home-ported at Saigon and then at Bombay. She was teamed with two similar-sized liner-troopships, Cunard's *Mauretania* and Holland America Line's *Nieuw Amsterdam*. With similar capacities and speeds, the three ships worked the Capetown–Suez troop shuttle. However, by 1943 the *Île* was called back to the North Atlantic, to be part of the enormous preparation for the D-Day invasion, which would come in June 1944. The *Île* had now switched over to Cunard Line management and carried a European staff. Her immediate fleetmates at the time included another French liner, the 1939-built *Pasteur*, which belonged to Compagnie de Sud-Atlantique.

The *Île* was a great survivor and witnessed the end of war in Europe in May 1945 and then in the Pacific three months later. During her five years of war service, she had steamed some 400,000 miles and transported 626,000 troops. She was decommissioned by the British in September and the 'heroic ship' officially returned to the French. But there was no time for a full refit. She was quickly repainted with her French Line red-and-black funnels and sent off on a busy round of austerity voyages – between Cherbourg and New York on the Atlantic (Le Havre had been heavily damaged during the war and needed clearing as well as rebuilding), some trips to Halifax and others out to far-off French colonial Indochina (often based at Marseille and usually sailing via the Suez Canal). Meanwhile, in Paris, both the French Government and the French Line were interested in resuming first-class passenger and mail service on the prestigious North Atlantic run to New York.

The French Line had actually resumed passenger service soon after the war officially ended, in May 1945, using the otherwise small, seventy-six-berth passenger-cargo ship *Oregon* and later another similar ship, *Wisconsin*. Two years later, in July 1947, they were joined by a passenger liner, the 17,700grt, 970-berth *De Grasse*. But ships such as *Oregon*, *Wisconsin* and even the liner *De Grasse* were temporary 'stopgaps'. The *Île* was much needed to restore the glamorously luxurious French Line service well remembered from before the war. Her first official post-war commercial trip was a sailing in April 1946 from Boston to Southampton and Cherbourg. With her hull and superstructure still in wartime grey, she carried a scant 186 passengers on that crossing, all of them in austere, wartime-like accommodations. Just before this trip she had crossed westbound to Halifax, bringing 7,000 Canadian soldiers home.

In the spring of 1947, the all-but-exhausted *Île* was fully returned to the French Line and then to St Nazaire for rebuilding. Optimistically, it was initially reported that she would be resuming service within a year or so. However, there were problems, including shortages of materials,

With only her forward funnel in place, the heavily worked *Île de France* is seen at St Nazaire about to undergo her post-Second World War refit and modernisation. This view dates from the spring of 1947. (Richard Faber Collection)

Nearing the end of her two-year refit, *Île de France* still needs her exterior painting in this scene from 1949. (Richard Faber Collection)

Another shipyard view of the incomplete *Île de France* in 1949. (Richard Faber Collection)

The combination passenger-cargo ship *Oregon* was used by the French Line to restore the Le Havre–New York service in May 1945. She could carry up to seventy-six passengers. (Richard Faber Collection)

sluggish efforts at the shipyard and, an ailment well known to the French, industrial strikes. Money was in short supply as well since the war had all but bankrupted the French. In the end, French Line designers and decorators had over two years, until the summer of 1949, to 'glamorise' *Île de France*. Alone, on the outside, her three funnels were removed and scrapped, and two wider, more streamlined funnels fitted instead. As times and demands had changed as well, the ship's berthing pattern was modernised to a more suitable 541 first class, 577 cabin class and 227 tourist class.

In January 1949, the French Line reported:

> The vessel's interior has been completely torn out, and steel deck and bulkhead plating laid bare throughout. The cabins, public rooms, crew's quarters, kitchens and storerooms are all being installed 'from scratch'. Even new dog kennels on the Sun Deck are being installed. In the ship's wine cellars, carpenters are fitting new, tilted bottle racks. Topside, the teak decks are being ripped out and fresh teak planks laid.

While extensive and thorough, the French did cut some costs with the reconditioning of the *Île*, it was later reported, because more and more monies were needed for the restoration of the larger *Liberté*. Robert Allan, an architect and ship enthusiast, noted: 'Many of the ceilings even in first-class cabins aboard the *Île de France* remained exposed. New flat, steel ceilings would have been too expensive and the overall budget for the refit of the ship had to be trimmed.'

Gleaming in fresh coats of paint and with her new look both inside and out (altogether said to cost $20 million), *Île de France* left Le Havre on her post-war maiden voyage on 21 July 1949. Six days later, escorted by harbour tugs, spraying fireboats, buzzing helicopters and even a US Navy blimp overhead, the handsome-looking *Île* slowly and graciously sailed into New York Harbour. The outbound liner *America*, then flagship of the US merchant fleet, gave her a rousing salute. Dressed in flags and to whistle salutes, the French ship was later berthed at Pier 88, at the foot of West 48th Street. The French Line, it seemed, was officially back in business and the *Île* was soon booked to capacity on every sailing. The Atlantic liner trade was regaining its stride, and business, including lots of summertime tourists, was growing. While the 23-knot *Île* aptly represented the French, sailing between Le Havre, Southampton or Plymouth and New York, Britain at that time had the largest and fastest liners, the legendary *Queen*

Inbound at New York on her first post-war crossing. (Moran Towing & Transportation Co.)

Return to service: *Île de France* steams across the English Channel from Le Havre to Southampton during her post-war maiden crossing, 21 July 1949. (Cronican-Arroyo Collection)

Escorted by tugs, small craft and spraying fireboats, the *Île* – with her more modern twin funnels – makes a triumphant return to service. (Cronican-Arroyo Collection)

Following her return to service, *Île de France* was again one of the most popular liners on the North Atlantic. (Cronican-Arroyo Collection)

Careful handling – during a New York tug strike, the *Île* slowly approaches the north side of Pier 88, 5 February 1953. (Richard Faber Collection)

During another tugboat strike, the mighty *Île de France* undocks herself. (Cronican-Arroyo Collection)

Mary and *Queen Elizabeth*, as well as *Britannic*, *Mauretania* and the brand-new *Caronia*; the aforementioned *America* carried the United States in regular service; the *Nieuw Amsterdam* was back for the Dutch; the Italians were, however, somewhat demoded with the smaller near-sisters *Saturnia* and *Vulcania*; and the once-mighty Germans were stripped and temporarily non-existent in trans-ocean liner service. On the horizon, all eyes seemed to be focused on the Americans, who began building a huge liner with 'secret power and amazing speed' which assuredly would make her the fastest liner afloat and most likely one of the most popular and successful. She would be, of course, the brilliant speed champion *United States* of 1952.

As the *Île* swung into her berth late in the afternoon of 27 July, 'the pier was jammed with greeters' welcoming the flag-bedecked ship. A long round of receptions, parties and dinners on board followed, including a luncheon for no less than 145 reporters and another for 250 travel agents. As *Île de France* docked, *Queen Mary* and *Mauretania* were at the adjoining pier. The deep whistles of the two Cunarders sounded out across the Hudson. They joined the welcome: an old marine friend had come back.

Newspapers were wildly enthusiastic in their praise of the restored liner. The *New York Times* noted: 'The secret of French-flag passenger ship operations has been an emphasis on excellent cuisine and service, but the refurbished *Île de France* has a third element – atmosphere.' The *New York Herald Tribune* paid equal tribute: 'The chapel is all that remains of the *Île*'s pre-war passenger installations. Now, the famed liner has been transformed into a vessel that surpasses even her former self in luxury, passenger comforts and technical improvements.'

Writer Horace Sutton was among her immediate fans:

The arrival of a reincarnate Madame Pompadour for an extended stay in New York would hardly create more of a stir among passengers of French elegance than the return of the *Île de France* to Manhattan harbor on July 27th, twenty-two years, one month and one day after her maiden voyage. To the international set who traveled with her for 346 crossings until she went to war in 1939, the *Île de France* was the quintessence of French taste. She was also the very finest example of modern interior ship design. She was bold. A nude figure called *Youth and Love*, which reposed modestly in the Salon Mixte, created such a transatlantic stir it was soon removed. The *Île* always had a singular personality that even the hulking *Normandie* never possessed, and a demure charm never duplicated by ships flying other national flags. In the words of a veteran traveler, the other lines doggedly 'gotcha there,' while it was a strict principle of French seamanship to avoid rough weather wherever possible. The French never liked it said they were actually at sea.

Mr Sutton continued:

From the very first, the *Île* was built as a yacht and run as a house-party boat. It drew the elegant – and those who could pay. The other lines who lost business to the *Île* regarded her with nautical scorn. 'What do they run it on,' was the disdainful question in shipping circles, 'champagne?'

As one habitué explained:

The French just 'applied love in every direction' to the *Île de France*. So many luminaries of public life flocked to the *Île* that some well-to-do and idle Americans would hire cabins for the entire summer and just ride back and forth. Three evenings out of six on every voyage were party nights, leaving three for recuperation.

'Even now, after the war, nobody in the French Line, especially aboard the *Île*, seems out of practice in the methods of handling a paying customer,' concluded Mr Sutton:

Every day, 122 cooks will prepare 54 items for lunch, 53 for dinner and offer eggs 14 different ways. For the maiden trip, the *Île* has purchased 20,000 lbs of beef, 4,000 fowl, 5,000 lbs of butter of which 3,000 will go for cooking and baking. And there are 5 bars on board, just in case anyone gets thirsty. Most of the important dissipation will take place in the Café de Paris, a glassed-in night club in first class. The sommelier has taken aboard – for the first run only – 5,600 bottles of champagne, 26,700 bottles of other wines and 4,000 gallons of wine for the crew. Overall, the ship's designer claims that the cabin-class accommodations

Ocean liner style! The superb, post-war main dining room in first class aboard the restored *Île de France*. (French Line)

The grand salon in first class. (French Line)

Glamour on the high seas! The cabin-class drawing room. (French Line)

Another view of the splendid grand salon in first class. (French Line)

The first-class writing room. (French Line)

The smoking room in first class. (French Line)

The ship's main foyer. (French Line)

The main dining room in tourist class. (French Line)

The writing room in cabin class. (French Line)

The main salon in tourist class. (French Line)

The superb library in first class. (French Line)

The bedroom of the Fontainebleu Suite, which included a sitting room, trunk room and full bathroom. It was priced from $1,200 per person for a six-night crossing to Le Havre in 1953. (Cronican-Arroyo Collection)

A twin-bedded first-class cabin. (Cronican-Arroyo Collection)

A single cabin with private veranda. (Cronican-Arroyo Collection)

The bedroom of the luxurious Compiegne Suite. (Cronican-Arroyo Collection)

A first-class cabin that is convertible to a sitting room by day.
(Cronican-Arroyo Collection)

An outside four-berth cabin in cabin class. The high season fare was $235
per person for a six-day crossing. (Cronican-Arroyo Collection)

Fun for all! The first-class children's playroom. (Cronican-Arroyo Collection)

The indoor swimming pool. (French Line)

The first-class gymnasium. (Cronican-Arroyo Collection)

The sun deck between the two funnels. (Cronican-Arroyo Collection)

Another view of the sun deck showing the aft funnel. (Cronican-Arroyo Collection)

are better than what was considered luxurious for first class ten years ago. Aside from ordinary cabins, the new ship has 30 suites, of which six are apartments de luxe, each named after a French chateau and decorated by a noted French artist. These apartments include a bedroom for two, a salon which can be converted into a double bedroom and a full bath. After all, it was not uncommon on the old Île for passengers to be accompanied by a butler, chef, masseur, nurse and doctor, not to mention furniture and mattresses. It is against the ship's rules to keep pets in the staterooms, but you can board your dog in heated kennels up on the sun deck. A special kennel menu, including a chef's daily special, is printed every day. Dog biscuits are freshly prepared and from an exclusive French Line recipe. Those pet menus are in French, by the way, which I suppose is in deference to French poodles.

For her maiden summer season, minimum fares were $345 in first class, $220 in cabin class and $165 in tourist class. Film stars, industrial tycoons and royalty (including lots of foreign royals like Queen Frederika of Greece and the exiled King of Yugoslavia) travelled aboard her. There were also lots of American families in cabin class, off on a summer in Europe or being transferred for business, but the less affluent budget tourists, along with teachers and students, opted for less expensive tourist class. 'It was often said in France that travelling in tourist class had a great attraction: shipboard romance,' said Philippe Brebant.

The Île settled down quickly to a happy, successful second career. She was as popular as ever. 'There was a certain cache to crossing to or from Europe aboard the Île de France,' commented Lewis Gordon, who crossed the Atlantic on over 100 voyages. 'Possibly even more so than the Liberté and certainly even more than, say, the two big Cunard Queens, the Île had this very select maritime persona. She had a select style. She had a certain ambience. She was chic. She was always fun. And of course she had the best cooks on the Atlantic.'

Peter Fialkowski recalled Île de France:

My memories of the Île de France date back to a crisp April 1st 1954 morning in New York when I was not quite six years old. As our taxi reached the docks, we first passed a couple of warships, then there she was, the magnificent Île with her almost exaggerated sheer rising to the top of the bow. (Later, I was to learn that the sheer at the bow was phony, and had been painted on to make the ship look more modern after the war.)

Due to my young age, I spent much of the time in the first-class children's play room way up on boat deck. While there weren't organised excursions for us, we did have a merry-go-round and Guignolle or puppet theatre manned by a crew member to keep us entertained. On one occasion, the stewardess in charge, who was dressed as a nurse, took us youngsters to the theatre to watch some cartoons. This, of course, was way before the days of videos and computer games. From time to time, my father would rescue me to catch a movie in the nearby movie theatre, which on another occasion served as a concert hall for a piano recital, often performed by one of the passengers who was a well-known musician.

Indeed passengers were far more interesting in those days, and on our crossing everyone seemed to be talking about our fellow passenger Lena Horne. Of course, I had no idea who Lena Horne was, but I recall my parents discreetly pointing out this very glamorous lady who was walking by. I was only permitted in the main dining room for breakfast, but I well recall the huge room with the Bas Reliefs of various French landmarks. Our crossing brought rather stormy weather and, by the

Celebrities at sea! Prince Rainier aboard *Île de France* in 1955. (Photofest)

Film star Lena Horne and her husband Lennie Hayton aboard the *Île* in September 1950. (Photofest)

Reclusive film queen Greta Garbo boards *Île de France* at Pier 88 in July 1949. (Photofest)

Princess Aga Khan poses aboard the *Île* during a crossing dated 30 March 1951. (Photofest)

third breakfast, the chinaware was all being supported in metal devices on the table to prevent them from sliding off. For other meals, I'd descend a long straight staircase to the children's dining room to join the other kids.

C.M. Squarey, a noted British travel writer, appraised passenger ships in the late 1940s and during the 1950s. He visited *Île de France* in September 1949 and was deeply impressed:

Here, indeed, is a romantic ship, a dramatic ship and a stately ship – romantic because of her reputation from pre-war times, dramatic because of her distinguished war record and stately because she portrays all the finest traits and characteristics, as well as the arts, of that history-steeped nation whose flag she flies so honourably today. This ship is so utterly and superbly French that one scarcely dares to talk, to write, about her in other than the French language …

Striding up what must be the world's longest gangway, I entered the Grand Foyer of this ship and, in two blinks, sensed that certain vitality

and zest for life that is a product of the French temperament and French way of living. Amongst other things that struck me were the bell boys in their smart red rig, the boulevard effect of the promenade deck with its rows of bright red deck chairs, the orchestra playing at embarkation time and the iced water laid around the ship.

And then one comes to food, and where food is supremely good, who can refrain from talking about it? Here are three subtle compliments: firstly, the French Line advertisement, 'It is harder to diet on the *Île de France* than any other ship'. I like that one. Secondly, an American onboard said to me, 'I don't know a French ship that isn't good – they don't know how to spoil good food.' There is a sting in that. Thirdly, there is the story about a press reporter asking the chef whether the liner's cuisine would be up to her high pre-war standard. 'Sir!' answered the chef indignantly, 'It will be the finest food in the world.' And then, to emphasise his point, he added, 'There are always more seagulls following the *Île de France* for scraps than any other ship on the ocean!'

The *Île* had, it was said, a very devoted, highly attentive crew and staff. 'At the French Line in the 1950s, crew members liked to be on the same ship. They didn't like to change from one ship to another, even between the two greatest liners, the *Île de France* and the *Liberté*,' recounted Philippe Brebant. 'The crews much preferred the New York run. It was faster, with quicker returns to France, and of course the tips were much better. If there was a problem with a crew member, they were sent to the Caribbean service, which was longer and of course far fewer tips.' Brebant added, 'During her final decade, seamen in her crew pleaded with company officials not to reassign them to other ships, including the *Liberté*.'

The *Île* also made headline news on several occasions in the remaining decade of her life. On 25–26 July 1956, while outbound from New York, she heroically rescued 753 survivors from the sinking liner *Andrea Doria*. The doomed, 3-year-old Italian flagship had been fatally rammed by another passenger ship, Sweden's *Stockholm*, off Nantucket. The disaster made headline news around the world and the *Île* gallantly played a most important role.

In her final decade, the *Île de France* developed an almost remarkable habit of rescuing and assisting other ships. She was soon dubbed 'the St Bernard of the Atlantic'. On Christmas Day 1951, she stood by the crippled British freighter *Chiswick* in heavy seas. In 1953, she stood by the sinking Liberian freighter *Greenville* and picked up her crew in raging waters. She also took on injured crew members of other smaller ships.

In October 1956, the *Île* was lashed by a violent North Atlantic storm. Six passenger cabins were flooded and the superstructure dented. Months later, in February 1957, she went aground during a winter Caribbean cruise at Fort de France on Martinique. The damages to the ship's hull were considerable. Her passengers were forced ashore and had to be flown home, while a sturdy, ocean-going tug was summoned to tow the liner to the big Newport News Shipyard in Virginia, the nearest facility capable of handling her in dry dock. The ship's schedules were, of course, disrupted, sailings cancelled and her passengers transferred to other ships.

New York-based transportation editor George Horne was a great fan of *Île de France* and wrote of that mishap in the Caribbean in 1957:

> The worst incident in the *Île*'s post-war life was in Martinique. With 786 passengers aboard, the ship, leaving the port, ran up on some rocks and damaged a rudder and two of her four propellers. The passengers had to be repatriated, but some of them, including several who had travelled on her many times, refused to leave. Listen to one of them: 'The company officials finally got us to leave, but we managed to stay aboard for 9 days, lying in Fort de France harbour. We loved that ship. She wasn't air-conditioned, and I've been aboard her in the Caribbean where the temperature was 100 degrees. But it made no difference. I would sail on her over and over as long as I live.'

Aged, creaking and moaning, *Île de France* turned 31 in 1958, just as commercial jet aircraft began its shattering intrusion over the Atlantic, with the first jets making their flights across the great ocean in October of that year. Their invasion and subsequent success was all but devastating to passenger shipping. Actual numbers were already slowly declining aboard Atlantic liners and even the impeccably reputed *Île* was no exception. In November, under sombre autumn skies and after 620 crossings, the *Île* left New York for the last time. A somewhat melancholy, even tearful crowd saw the ship off at Pier 88. Moran tugs eased her out, positioned for the southward sail along the Hudson, and blasts on her mighty steam whistles signalled the final goodbye to Manhattan, a place she had known since that very first visit back in 1927.

Rumours and schemes soon surfaced regarding her future. One quarter wanted her for use as a hotel moored on the Riviera. The Sheraton Corporation was said to be even more prominent: they reportedly wanted her for use as a hotel on Martinique in the Caribbean. Another plan was to cut her masts, trim her funnels and reduce her superstructure for bridge clearance so that she could be towed along the Seine and brought into the heart of Paris. But in the end, it was about sheer economics. The French Line appeared pleased to accept a firm offer from a Japanese firm that wanted her for scrapping. Her end seemed assured – even if in some far-off scrapyard.

George Horne was mournful when news of her retirement was fixed:

> She is doomed now, called in with sad finality from the sea lanes she served so gallantly for 31 years, bound for the auction block and the un-tender probings of the wrecker. It is disquieting to think of the *Île de France* as scrap. She was a lady of quality. Not aloof, not stiff, not cool, not even possessing the appearance of snobbishness as protective covering. Instead, she had warmth, loveliness and a hospitality unmatched. And she had even more, an indefinable something that won a strange kind of fealty and adoration from her crew and from travellers, many of whom have time and again literally twisted their sailing schedules to voyage in the *Île*, not quite knowing why …
>
> The *Île de France* really gave the French Line its successful slogan: 'The Longest Gangplank in the world'. Once aboard the *Île*, one was in Paris. And the *Île* was destined to make news. Ship reporters like me made many friends aboard her, among crew and passengers. There was always news because there was always interesting people aboard like Helen Morgan, Ignace Paderewski, Lila Damita, Will Rogers, Gilbert Miller, Maurice Chevalier, Rachmaninoff, Chaliapin. Everyone travelled on the *Île*. We would move from cabin to cabin or, with the guidance of some bell boys, bring select passengers down to the children's playroom or dining room where we breakfasted and then interviewed at the same time people like Tallulah Bankhead, Marlene Dietrich, Gloria Swanson and Pavlova. Onboard, there were also bankers, politicians, statesmen, literary men, mountebanks and likeable rogues.

The waterfront at Le Havre was crowded with well-wishers when the *Île* departed for Osaka on 26 February 1959. Her stewards and seamen stood on the quayside and reportedly wept unashamedly. Under the command of a small Japanese crew, she hoisted the Japanese flag when at sea and was renamed *Furansu Maru* (France Maru). But any fears at the French Line offices back in Paris were soon realised when her shipbreaking owners chartered the famed ship to a Hollywood film company, at the rate of $4,000 per day, for use as a floating prop in the disaster-style production, *The Last Voyage*. It was a story based on the final sailing of a transpacific ship, the fictional *Claridon*. The French quickly went to court and succeeded in having her French Line funnel colours at least partially repainted and barred the use of her famous name.

In the lingering light of an autumn afternoon, *Île de France* departs from New York for the last time in this view dated November 1958. (Cronican-Arroyo Collection)

Ready to sail! The thunderous whistles signal another departure for Europe, but in the twilight of *Île de France*'s career. The date is 1957 and the ship will be retired by the end of the following year. (Moran Towing & Transportation Co.)

As seen from Pier 88, the silhouette of *Île de France* as she sails along the Hudson River for the last time. (Cronican-Arroyo Collection)

The *Île* had actually been sold to two Japanese firms: Mitsubishi Shoji and Okada-Gumi. They agreed later to lease the ship to Metro-Goldwyn Mayer. Andrew Stone, the director-producer, first wanted the *Arundel Castle*, a 20,000grt, twin-funnel Union-Castle liner that was sold to Hong Kong scrappers in January 1959. But the filming schedule did not quite work. *Île de France* was the next choice, being due in Japanese waters in March. Stone himself conceived *The Last Voyage*, the story of an aged Pacific liner on her final crossing that meets disaster. A father (Robert Stack) saves his wife (Dorothy Malone) and daughter (Tammy Merrihugh), and the film also tells the tale of a captain-host (George Saunders) whose gracious table manners hide his poor seamanship. But it was the ship itself that soon garnered all the publicity.

With *Liberté* in the background, *Île de France* is already flying the Japanese flag and preparing to depart from Le Havre for Osaka, 25 February 1959. (Philippe Brebant Collection)

French Line officials became disturbed, however, when they learned that the Japanese scrap firm would allow an undignified, explosive death for the much-beloved liner. They tried to restrict the filming. Mr Stone eventually agreed to a contract that prohibited him from using actors with French accents, referring to the French Line or even mentioning *Île de France*. The French Line demanded that all French signs had to be removed from filming sequences.

Mr Stone, with technical advisors aboard, exploded parts of the engine room, blew holes in several decks and allowed a piano to fall through one of the holes. Part of the forward bulkhead was blown out, permitting 300 tons of water to rush in. In the end, the pre-cut forward funnel was toppled on to the wheelhouse. For the explosive scenes, the steel sections were removed and replaced with plywood. There were lots of problems, of course. A Japanese artist was hired to repaint the lounge walls with Chinese fairy tales, for example, but in a misunderstanding he painted the *Arabian Nights* instead. While Mr Stone wanted to flood the forward part of the ship so that the propellers in the stern would lift out of the water, this was not allowed, especially by insurance officials. The carefully arranged flooding of the liner was done in fairly shallow waters off Osaka.

With actor Robert Stack in the foreground, evacuation scenes are being filmed aboard *Claridon*, the fictional name for *Île de France* in the making of the 1959 film *The Last Voyage*. (Photofest)

For the closing scene, as the ship sinks, MGM bought an old Japanese freighter with a similar wood superstructure.

Eventually, when the filming was complete, the former *Île de France* returned to Osaka for final demolition. Within months, she was reduced to rubble. Her reputation has remained, however, and she is widely regarded as one of the most important liners of the twentieth century.

4

FLAGSHIP OF THE FLEET: *LIBERTÉ*

When *Île de France* was 1½ years old, in the autumn of 1928, another great and important liner was launched. However, the ceremonies took place miles away from French soil, at the Blohm & Voss shipyard in Hamburg. She was the second of a pair of German superliners, both intended to be the fastest ships afloat. She was named *Europa* and, in the ironies of fate and history, she would one day be the running mate of *Île de France*. She would become the post-Second World War flagship of France, the *Liberté*. There were also times in the 1930s when the French *Île de France* and the German *Europa* were together at New York, in adjoining berths at Piers 86 and 88.

The Germans, namely the North German Lloyd, were making an almost phenomenal resurgence following the devastating losses of the First World War with not one but two superliners within the following decade. *Europa* and her near-sister *Bremen* were due to have a grand debut. Both liners were scheduled to enter service on 1 April 1929 and then sail as a pair to New York. Furthermore, as two of the world's largest and most luxurious liners, they were expected to capture the prized Blue Riband, taking it from Britain and Cunard's *Mauretania*, the proud holder for some twenty-two years. But there were serious problems and then misfortune. A major strike at Blohm & Voss lasted for three months, starting in October 1928. *Europa's* delivery was no longer guaranteed. Then there was a far more serious worry. Fire broke out on board the incomplete liner on 25 March 1929. The blaze spread quickly, destroying and even buckling the upper-deck areas. Some 350 firemen using 65 hoses fought the blaze well into the next day. Initial appraisals concluded that the brand-new liner was a loss and might have to be scrapped. Flooded with firefighters' water, she soon settled at her shipyard berth. Fortunately, further investigations

and studies suggested that the 936ft-long ship could be saved and so, on 10 April, she was raised and major repairs soon commenced. The ship was delayed by another ten months.

The fire was all but faded in memory when *Europa* left Bremerhaven on 30 March 1930, crossing to New York in six days with stops en route at Southampton and Cherbourg. She was pleasing in every way, having a record speed of 27.9 knots and thereby surpassing her near-sister *Bremen's* top speed of 27.8 knots. *Europa* promptly captured the Blue Riband. After changes to her steam-turbine machinery, the slightly larger *Bremen* recaptured the Riband in June 1933 with a recorded speed of 28.5 knots. Two months later, the record passed to Italy's *Rex*. In the late 1930s, following the subsequent speed successes of France's *Normandie* and Britain's *Queen Mary*, and prodded by the Nazi Government, thought was given to re-engining both *Bremen* and *Europa*, thereby giving them even greater speeds. The idea soon passed by and instead plans were drawn for two bigger, very powerful superliners. But these, too, were abandoned, especially as military plans by the Nazis had far greater priority.

Soon after their maiden voyages, the initial flat, squat funnels proved problematic, with smoke and soot disturbing passengers on the upper, open decks. The funnels on both ships were raised. At the same time, a Lufthansa seaplane resting in a revolving catapult was fitted to the top deck of both ships. Approximately forty hours before reaching either side of the Atlantic, the plane was loaded with mail and dispatched ahead, creating something of a 'fast' sea-mail service. It was a publicity touch, but also a costly, awkward one. By 1935, the plane and catapult were removed.

While acclaimed and indeed high points of German international public relations, neither *Bremen* nor *Europa* were great financial successes.

The mighty *Europa* as built in 1930 with her low, squat funnels; these were soon raised to reduce the smoke and soot falling on passengers on the open, outer decks below. (Hapag-Lloyd)

Deeper into the 1930s, and while popular with many Germans, the two ships lost more and more passengers due to rising anti-Nazi feelings, especially in the United States. By 1938–39, they had all but lost completely the important American Jewish market. In February 1939, *Bremen*'s long, luxurious cruise around South America was a flop, sailing with less than 200 passengers.

In 1939, German ships, including *Europa*, were closely watched as centres of Nazi propaganda in the United States. Crew members reportedly attended pro-Nazi meetings while the ships were berthed along Manhattan's West Side. Among passengers, and as the Nazi war march became more apparent, the popularity of *Europa* as well as *Bremen* dropped even further.

Europa was used mostly for Atlantic crossings: six days between Bremerhaven and New York, five days from Southampton and Cherbourg. The 49,746grt ship was divided into four classes: 687 first class, 524 second class, 306 tourist class and 507 third class. By 1937, peak summer season fares were shown as being from $267 in first class (then called cabin class) between New York and Bremerhaven, and $146 in cabin class (then called tourist class) and $106 in tourist class (then referred to as third class).

Passengers boarding *Europa* at the Columbus Quay at Bremerhaven in a view dated 1935. (Hapag-Lloyd)

An advertisement dated December 1935. (National Geographic Society)

Europa is just arriving at New York's Pier 86 in this grand view of Luxury Liner Row, 18 April 1939. From top to bottom are: *Conte di Savoia*, *Georgic*, *Queen Mary*, *Paris*, *De Grasse* and *New York*. (Author's Collection)

Ultimately, war for the Nazis was close at hand. On a westbound crossing in late August 1939, *Europa* was suddenly ordered to reverse course and return to Bremerhaven. The Nazi invasion of Poland was but days away. Blacked out and with radio silence, she sped to home waters and offloaded her worried, greatly inconvenienced passengers. Once Britain and France officially declared war on Germany, on 3 September, she was repainted in military grey and used as a naval accommodation ship at Bremerhaven. In 1940, together with *Bremen*, she sailed to nearby Hamburg for intended conversion to a huge landing ship, with large doors to be cut in her sides, for the projected Nazi invasion of Britain. Within a short time, however, the idea was abandoned and both ships returned to

Bremerhaven. *Bremen* was destroyed there by fire in March 1941 while rumours circulated that *Europa* would soon be converted to a large aircraft carrier. This plan never came to pass either.

While still the largest ship in the German fleet by the war's end in May 1945, *Europa* was a neglected, rusting sight when American invasion forces reached Bremerhaven. Fortunately, she survived the war, remained afloat and was spared from Allied bombings. There were orders at the end from the retreating Nazi High Command to sink her, but these were never carried out. On board, there was some evidence of alterations and provisions for troops that never came aboard. She was officially seized as a prize of war on 8 May by a US Navy captain and twenty-four American bluejackets. After this she was placed under the US flag and designated AP-177, USS *Europa*. At the time of capture, Captain Oskar Scharf, her pre-war master, was aboard along with several other North German Lloyd officers and about 100 German seamen. It was obvious to the American boarding party that maintenance throughout the war had been, at best, haphazard. 'Years of accumulated dust lay over her once luxurious interiors,' reported a member of the invasion forces.

In the 16 May 1945 edition of the *New York Times*, it was reported: 'The American flag or the White Ensign of the Royal Navy has been hoisted over 475 German naval and merchant ships including the transatlantic liner *Europa*. The *Europa* was found at Bremerhaven in relatively good condition, although she has been silted in. Recently, she has been used as a German naval barracks.'

Europa was soon moved to dry dock, to a nearby shipyard in Bremerhaven, as reported in the news of 6 June. Said to be worth $16 million at the time, she had been stripped of most of her luxurious fittings and was undamaged except for a small bomb, which was dropped during a Royal Air Force raid in 1940. The bomb landed between the ship's two funnels and two steel beams were bent. Otherwise, damages were minimal. With determined efforts by shipyard crews, the ship would be ready, it was estimated, by mid-September. Some 2,300 workers were used for the reactivation and reconditioning of *Europa*, with many of them recruited by American forces from Nazi prison camps. She would be used as a much-needed, high-capacity American troopship. Captain Scharf and seventy-nine other former crew members had volunteered for sea duty when *Europa* returned to the sea. Within days, however, American seamen's unions protested against the German staffing of the ship under the US flag and their efforts included a direct appeal to President Truman in Washington.

During July, and with much of Germany in ruins, it was reported that the reconditioning and dry docking of *Europa* was well under way and the ship was found to be in 'relatively good condition'. The ship's twelve turbines, the rudder and the shaftings required additional overhauling. A further report in the *New York Times* dated 22 July noted:

Orders were received today [from US Navy headquarters in Washington] to make the conversion of the *Europa* into a troop transport as a No. 1 priority job. Paint was being flown from England to give the ship a new battleship-gray dress. During her first month of dry docking, tons of barnacles had been scraped off. These collected during the liner's four years' 'imprisonment' in the Kaiserlauten slip [at Bremerhaven].

After a long wartime lay-up, *Europa* is moved out of dry dock at Bremerhaven to begin duties carrying Allied troops as a US flag transport, 17 September 1945. (Cronican-Arroyo Collection)

On 26 August, USS *Europa* was officially commissioned as a US Navy transport. Some 800 navy officers and men – the entire crew from another troop transport, USS *Monticello* (the former Italian liner *Conte Grande*) – would form the ship's company. Captain Benjamin Franklin Perry was named master.

There were troubles a day later, on 27 August. Five fires started almost simultaneously on *Europa*. There was little damage, however, and the fires were extinguished quickly. An American sailor attached to the ship was found to be the culprit – a 'firebug', as the US Navy called him.

As the summer of 1945 drew to a close, there were rumours, discussions and extended speculation that USS *Europa* was to be transferred from the US Navy to the War Shipping Administration, an agency which had more to do with post-war merchant shipping. There were further suggestions and even reports in the American press that *Europa* might be much like another German liner, *Vaterland*, which was seized in 1917 and became *Leviathan*, an American troopship transformed into a peacetime liner. She

The USS *Europa* at sea, carrying returning soldiers to New York. (Cronican-Arroyo Collection)

4,314 returning American soldiers. Among the more noticeable alterations aboard the ship was that German nameplates and instruction signs had been removed and changed to English. Thorough repairs and further conversion of the ship would be done in an American shipyard due to material shortages in war-torn Germany, however. At Southampton, Captain Scharf was seen aboard, looking 'somewhat dejected'. He and eight German technicians were being taken to New York as 'advisors' to the US Navy during further conversion work.

On 23 September 1945, the *New York Times* wrote extensively of *Europa*'s anticipated arrival in two days' time. It was the ship's first visit to New York in six years, since 23 August 1939. She was dubbed 'the biggest prize of war in shipping history' and it was said that she would most likely become 'the largest, fastest and most luxurious liner under the American flag'. At this time there had been no official decision to build the 53,300grt superliner that would become the record-breaking *United States*. That decision was made a year later, with construction beginning in 1948 and the 990ft-long vessel being commissioned in the summer of 1952.

After a storm-tossed crossing from Southampton, the delayed *Europa* docked at Pier 88 at nine in the evening on 24 September. She was given a whistle-blowing salute and welcome from other vessels and small craft in the harbour, but was unable to respond. Her once throaty steam whistles needed further repairs, it appeared. There was a welcoming ceremony once the ship was docked, but to which Captain Scharf and the other Germans were not invited to attend. A navy official called them 'passengers'. Her US Navy captain praised her performance at sea, saying 'she behaved beautifully'. She averaged 20 knots and, on two occasions, reached 23 knots. But an onlooker recalled the sight of the once impeccable German superliner: 'Her long sides were so stained that the deep grey appeared to be black. Her twin funnels seemed only a little cleaner. In all, she appeared to be a battered ship.'

The ship was soon moved, within New York Harbour, for a forty-five-day refit in the 1,100ft-long US Navy graving dock at Bayonne, New Jersey. During this time, further information of her wartime period was revealed. It seems that the ship had been moved not once but twice from Bremerhaven to Hamburg, in 1940 and 1941, and that Hamburg shipyard crews had cut large boarding ports in her sides, apparently for use in landing invasion troops quickly in the assault on England. But they were soon closed up and the ship returned to Bremerhaven. In February 1945, *Europa* was officially transferred to the German navy for use as a receiving station for refugees from East and West Prussia. When the Americans seized the ship on 8 May, a large number of refugees were living aboard the otherwise idle liner.

sailed in US flag service until 1934 and then was scrapped four years later. Therefore, it was said that *Europa* might eventually be converted into America's largest luxury liner, a key element in 'the revival of American sea travel'. Meanwhile, there was some discussion that, under reparations pacts and agreements, the ship might be given to the British. There were hints that she could be allocated to Canadian Pacific as a replacement for their 42,000grt *Empress of Britain*, which was sunk by the Nazis in 1940. Alternately, it was hinted that she might be assigned to Cunard as a replacement for their aged *Aquitania*, which dated from 1914. There was further discussion which said that the United States had already 'reaped rich rewards', with enemy transports and especially four ex-Italian liners – *Saturnia*, *Vulcania*, *Conte Biancamano* and *Conte Grande* – being in American hands.

Belching huge amounts of thick black smoke and with the channel near Bremerhaven specially dredged, *Europa* left her German home port on 11 September and headed for Southampton, where she would load

However, perhaps most significant of all, the German High Command had ordered the destruction of the ship on 7 May, the day before she was seized by the invading American forces. The order was rescinded, for unexplained reasons, only hours before the Americans boarded the ship.

Only weeks into her refit at Bayonne, in October, it was decided to reduce the conversion and instead leave some of her interiors suitable for reconditioning as a luxury passenger liner, possibly sailing for the United States Lines on the North Atlantic. There was a plan to increase her troop capacity from 4,500 to as many as 10,000, but this was reconsidered for 5,000 or 6,000 soldier-passengers, thereby leaving some of her original German accommodations intact. The travel section of the *New York Times* dated 7 October 1945 suggested: 'The former German liner *Europa* might be the first big luxury ship to go into American transatlantic passenger service.'

With the overall reconditioning plans scaled down, *Europa* left the Bayonne graving dock on 7 November, moved to Pier 88 in Manhattan and soon began regular trooping duties. She sailed on the 11th with forty-four passengers aboard, no troops and 960 in her crew. One report at the time stated: 'The less extensive conversion on the *Europa* will make reconversion for ordinary transatlantic liner service and under the American flag much easier and less costly.' The Bayonne refit did include the fitting of an additional 4,000 standee bunks on B and C decks and the installation of tier bunks in staterooms. Some 800 bunks were installed in the first-class main lounge. Several public rooms were converted to mess halls. The ship was also equipped with fire-protection devices. Sprinklers were installed and some of the wiring, faulty by US Coast Guard inspection standards, was replaced. All but four of the ship's large lifeboats were removed to lessen the upper weight on the superstructure. Life rafts placed on the open decks could, it was estimated, handle up to 9,000 in an emergency. Otherwise, a navy spokesman noted that the ship's beautiful mural decorations, including the gold and tile mosaic in the lounge, were untouched and the bronze statue depicting the legend of *Europa* was still in place.

Carrying large loads of troops on her westbound voyages, *Europa*'s eastbound crossings were offered to passengers and booked by the United States Lines. On 30 November 1945, for example, the ship departed with sixty passengers aboard. 'Passengers will travel comfortably and safely enough to Southampton,' said a US Navy spokesman. 'But on the way, they will clean their own dishes, put their utensils and mess gear in proper places and make and keep their cabins shipshape. Dining is cafeteria style.' A United States Lines agent added: 'We stopped short of asking them to bring along their own carpet sweepers!'

In reality, the US Navy was unhappy with the ship. More specifically, top navy officials, it was reported, were 'vastly uncomfortable' with *Europa*. Rumours were strong that she was unsafe and at risk. She had structural problems and faulty, substandard wiring. She appealed, it seemed, to no one in Washington and was called 'the problem ship' and dubbed a 'hot potato'. In late December she had further repairs at the Todd Shipyard, just across the Hudson in Hoboken, New Jersey, costing $100,000. By January, it was widely reported that the United States would 'wash its hands' of the 16-year-old vessel, possibly transfer her to the British or, more likely, pass her to the United Nations Shipping Pool for reassignment. The Soviet Union wanted passenger ships, and might have been tempted to buy her had it not been for the size of *Europa*. It seems, however, that American companies such as the United States Lines were still very much interested. But on 25 February, the US Navy formally rejected the ship, planning to send her back to Bremerhaven and place her in the hands of a reparations agency.

The intended 5 March sailing for USS *Europa* from New York to Bremerhaven was cancelled unexpectedly and then further delayed by eight days. The rumour along the New York waterfront was that the ship had 'big problems'. En route to Germany, she was sent farther north, routed above the isles of Scotland, and had to await sailing orders through the still-perilous North Sea minefields.

A week later, on 13 March, the Cabinet of the French Government in Paris was reportedly divided as to whether to ask for a replacement for *Normandie* as part of post-war reparations. Some ministers were anxious to resume tourist service between the United States and France, and generate income and exchange for a badly wounded French nation. The French could hardly afford to build a brand-new liner, and *Europa* fit the size requirements. Two months later it was officially announced in Washington that neither the US Government nor any American shipping interests wanted *Europa* or the cut-down, salvaged remains of *Normandie*. It was estimated, according to the final evaluations, that restoring *Normandie* would cost $30 million and reconditioning *Europa* at least $15 million.

A report not released until November 1946, and long after *Europa* was out of American hands, 'indicted' the pre-war Germans 'for permitting the operation of the liner *Europa* with low safety standards'. *Europa*, the report stated, was rushed to completion (in 1929–30) without adequate safety provisions after a final change in plans that increased the length and tonnage of the vessel from approximately 35,000 tons and 775ft in length. The report confirmed that after only three years of operations, by 1933, 'serious cracks' had developed in the ship and yet only minor repairs had been made. The ship was thereafter far below American safety standards. The ship continued, it appears, by relying on careful operation and seamanship. Furthermore, the ship's electrical installations constituted a 'serious fire hazard'.

Days later, also in May 1946, after the US officially said *Europa* was 'not wanted', the Inter-Allied Reparations Agency met in Brussels, voted quickly and awarded *Europa* and six other smaller German ships to the French. The French had, in fact, initially rejected or at least lost interest in *Europa*, professing that the country needed smaller, more useful vessels, namely important cargo ships. However, soon afterwards, the US Government allocated seventy-five Liberty ships to the French and this changed their thinking rapidly. *Europa* now had far greater potential, especially in restoring liner services. Things moved forward, and very quickly. On 20 May, it was strongly rumoured that the ship, lying at Bremerhaven under the watchful eye of a small caretaker crew, would become *La Libération*, a name soon reportedly changed to *Libération*. However, by 30 May, the naming was changed again, this time to *La Lorraine*. Nevertheless, there had been no formal renaming when, on 10 June, a French crew was sent to Bremerhaven to collect the ship. She was brought to Cherbourg, where she docked on 15 June and then

quickly went into a local dry dock for initial repairs and the start of her conversion back to a luxury liner. After this it was rumoured that she would be renamed *La Liberté*.

Guy de Berc, general manager in North America for the French Line, held a press conference thoughtfully on 3 July 1946. He announced then that *Europa* would now be renamed *Liberté* and that, with proper reconditioning, she would be in Le Havre–New York service that November and sailing in company with the rebuilt but far smaller *De Grasse*. He also predicted that, while 'the *Liberté* will not emerge as a typical French Line vessel' and luxury passenger service was not yet a national priority, *Île de France* would join them in the summer of 1947 and thereby, with three ships, create a weekly service in each direction. He added that the three ships would create a 'de luxe stop gap' service for four or five years until the French Line's 'new construction program' could get under way. He also added that cruises in the winter, off-season, would not be resumed until 1948 or 1949. Just prior to de Berc's announcements, Jean Marie, the president of CGT (the French Line) at its headquarters in Paris, enthusiastically announced the 'planning and construction' of no less than seven new liners which, he claimed, would be somewhere in size between the 28,000-ton, pre-war *Champlain* and the 43,500-ton *Île de France*. The three ships, he reported with great confidence, would be

Handed over to the French, the funnels of the former *Europa* have already been repainted in the French Line's colours of red and black, November 1946. (Author's Collection)

Renamed *Liberté*, the 936ft-long ship waits at Le Havre to be moved to St Nazaire for a full, extended conversion into the new French Line flagship. (Author's Collection)

for the prestigious New York run. Claiming also that French shipyards had returned to 70 per cent of their pre-war production levels, France was, as he worded his closing, 'on the way back'.

In a subsequent announcement, the CGT president added that *Liberté* was found, despite earlier American evaluations, to be in very good condition, that her general passenger layout would be unchanged, but that she would be 'brightened up and modernised' overall. The formal renaming of the ship was held at Cherbourg on 27 July. Dignitaries attended, Le Havre had been painted on the stern, the funnels repainted in the French Line's signature red and black, and a large Tricolour unfurled off the starboard stern. It was a positive occasion for the press – the French liner fleet was being revived! Diplomatically after the ship's transfer to the French, American authorities were publicly far less critical of the ship's condition, stating: 'We understand that the French are taking great steps to improve the ship's earlier condition.'

However, neither de Berc nor Marie's predictions held firm or true. *Liberté* would not be in service by the autumn of 1946, but would instead return almost four years later, in the summer of 1950; *De Grasse* would be delayed by at least half a year, until the summer of 1947; and *Île de France* would not resume luxury sailing in 1947, but two years later, in the summer of 1949. Also, as to the seven large liners, it was not until 1950 that only two liners were planned, and these were comparatively smaller, at 20,000 tons each.

There were other, quite serious worries when, on 8 December, *Liberté* was nearly lost. Moved to Le Havre for further reconditioning, the port was lashed by a storm of record fury. The storm was said to be the worst in Le Havre's history and had all but crippled shipping in the English Channel. The gales were ferocious. *Liberté*'s steel mooring cables were snapped one by one. She was soon ripped from her moorings and, adrift, slammed into the bow of the sunken wreckage of the liner *Paris*, which had burned and capsized at her French Line berth in April 1939. The wreck had not been removed, even in almost eight years, because of the war. A great hole was ripped into the starboard side of *Liberté*; her lower decks were soon awash in high tide and she was pounded relentlessly by the waves. Settling on a mud bank in 7 fathoms of water, *Liberté* soon listed as much as 37 degrees. Even part of the promenade deck was under water. The crew had quickly abandoned the ship.

On the morning of the 9th, tugs came to the rescue, and with the rising tide, fortunately righted the liner and reduced her list to only 5 degrees. Nearby, another French ship, *Palmyre*, was ripped from her moorings, from which she began to drift and collided with a US Navy launch, sinking

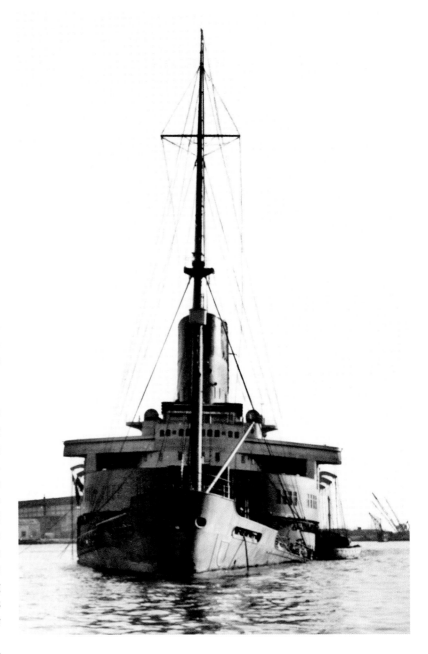

After being lashed during a fierce Atlantic storm on 9 December 1946, *Liberté* was ripped from her moorings, rammed the sunken remains of the liner *Paris*, flooded and then canted over. She then righted but was allowed to settle upright. (French Line)

This view, dated 10 December 1946, shows *Liberté* resting in the mud at Le Havre. Everything below C deck is underwater. (Cronican-Arroyo Collection)

In this view across the bow of *Liberté*, the capsized wreck of the liner *Paris* can be seen. Burned out and capsizing in April 1939, it was not removed until 1947. (French Line)

it. The French Government created an immediate inquiry into the event, but was quick to rule out sabotage in the case of *Liberté*. Insured for $5 million, the loss of *Liberté* would have been a great setback to the French Line. The ship might have been a complete loss, worthy only of the scrappers, but divers inspected her underwater damages and determined that she could be saved and repaired. However, the latest time schedule for getting the reconditioned liner into Atlantic service, set for May 1947, was again postponed. The next problem was that the huge ship now needed urgent and extended time in a dry dock. The nearby dry docks in Le Havre seemed ideal, but had been damaged in the war, and they themselves needed urgent repairs. Weeks later, in a statement made on 1 January 1947, the French announced that *Liberté* would be repaired and would enter service 'sometime in 1948'.

By 30 January, divers at Le Havre were busily plugging the hole in *Liberté*'s hull. But there were assorted complications. The port of Le Havre wanted to return to normalcy with regards to its shipping. Wreckage from the war had to be cleared, terminals rebuilt, docks reopened and the harbour waters cleared and dredged. The wreckage of the capsized, burnt-out *Paris* had to be finally removed, but the half-sunken *Liberté* blocked that process. Pumping out the big liner took on a new sense of

priority and two US Army floating docks were moored alongside to retain stability. Once *Liberté* could be moved safely, a Marseille-based salvage firm planned to cut up *Paris* into five sections, raising each of them and then scrapping them. By April, *Liberté* was patched, 75,000 cubic yards of water had been pumped out and she was all but refloated. Then, after some preliminary dry docking at Le Havre, it was decided that she would be sent to St Nazaire for extended reconditioning. That too was much delayed, however. She remained in Le Havre for another ten months, not departing (and under her own power) for St Nazaire until mid-November. But another huge Channel storm delayed things yet again and schedules and projections had to be reset. The rebuilt *De Grasse* would enter service that summer while *Liberté* and *Île de France* were now scheduled for November and December 1948.

There continued to be problems, however. Materials and supplies were in short supply in post-war France. There was a lack of steel. Then there were strikes, seemingly countless industrial actions by the shipyard workers, the crews and, of course, the dockers. The French Line had to realign their plans once more. *Île de France* now became the priority. She was reportedly 'stripped to the bone' and would be a virtually new ship when she resumed commercial service, though she was now rescheduled

Liberté has been moved to St Nazaire and is in dry dock in this view from 1948. (Richard Faber Collection)

for mid-1949. Meanwhile, also at St Nazaire, *Liberté* required much more attention, it seemed, and so was delayed until mid-1950.

Work on the two liners was at its peak in January 1949. Some 3,000 workers were attending to the two liners, but they were quite different projects. *Île de France* was all but gutted and being made over, whereas *Liberté* had to be largely 'effaced of her alien decorative scheme and tone, erasing the heavy and sombre Teutonic style'. The majority of the workers, 2,000 in all, were assigned to the *Île* and worked on twenty-four-hour day and night shifts.

Then there was another close call. While in dry dock at St Nazaire on 18 October 1949, a fire broke out aboard *Liberté*. Some sixty first-class cabins were damaged.

Liberté was finally due to leave Le Havre on 26 September 1950 on her post-war maiden voyage from Le Havre to New York. However, after yet another strike was settled, some 2,500 artisans and workers – with performance bonuses hanging in the balance – seemed to work overtime. The ship was actually ready a month early and could now offer two additional Atlantic roundtrips and thus would arrive in New York on 23 August. The final tab for the liner's three-year transformation was an expensive $19.5 million.

Reportedly, the French Line 'ripped out' everything in the liner that did not meet the latest 1948 Safety at Sea Standards. The extended refit was required to attend to every last detail. There were still occasional references, especially in the American press, to her defects as *Europa* – the structural weakness, the inadequacy of her compartmentation and her faulty, substandard electrical system. In order to lessen the strain longitudinally, the 'strength deck' was reinforced on the promenade by the addition of 'doubling' plates on either side. The extensive plate-strengthening covered half of the ship's 936ft length. To lighten the ends of the ship for increased strength and stability, water tanks forward were transformed into void spaces, and other water ballast tanks aft were emptied. In four midships tanks, 2,500 tons of ballast were added. Overall, these reduced stress, giving *Liberté* a strength component equal to the earlier *Normandie*, which was considered a very strong vessel. Fireproofing was also increased by replacing lots of wood fittings with metals. The fire-detection system now included seventy-five warning signals and 1,320 automatic fire detectors in passenger and crew spaces, even in storerooms. The ship's electrical power system was replaced and was 60 per cent greater than before the war.

Her passenger quarters expectedly attracted the greatest attention. Guy de Berc was aboard the trial trip as well as the inaugural crossing. He reported:

The two-deck-high first-class dining room under renovation and restoration in 1948–49. (Cronican-Arroyo Collection)

Nearing the completion of her long three-and-a-half-year refit, *Liberté* is seen in this view at Le Havre dated May 1950. (Cronican-Arroyo Collection)

In the final stages, *Liberté*'s refit is almost complete, 19 July 1950. (Cronican-Arroyo Collection)

To welcoming salutes, *Liberté* arrives at Le Havre for the first time since being rebuilt and refitted, 8 August 1950. (Cronican-Arroyo Collection)

French architects had made liberal use of glass and plastic in the public rooms and suites onboard. For instance, a passenger standing in the Winter Garden Bar forward has a clear view of activities on the stage of the theatre almost a ship-length away. In between are the Library, Salon and Smoking Room, all partitioned by glass. Artists have attempted to impart to the 16 suites a definite French decor and have carried the same theme of decorations, tapestries and other appointments of the public rooms in all classes. There is also a great sense of concentration. The First Class Gymnasium is on the same deck as the swimming pool and both are surrounded by steam, rest and massage rooms. All three dining rooms – for First Class, Cabin Class and Tourist Class – are on one deck and served by a single kitchen. Cabin and Tourist Class accommodations have been designed with a liberal amount of interchangeable space to allow for seasonal fluctuations. Cabin Class offers accommodations for 1–4 persons and Tourist Class 2–4. Pullman type beds in Cabin Class fold into the ceiling while those in Tourist Class disappear into the wall. Designers have particular attention to Cabin Class facilities. These include a gymnasium, Saloon, Smoking Room and children's Dining Room and Play Room. About one-third of the Sun Deck is designated for Cabin Class passengers, who may also alternate with First Class passengers in use of the ship's theatre. Bars, a Smoking Room and Saloon have also been provided for Tourist Class recreation.

When *Liberté* first arrived at Le Havre, a strong police guard surrounded and protected the ship. Visitor passes were strictly scrutinised, including those for the 1,000 workers that had sailed with the ship and were completing the final tasks. There was a distinct fear of sabotage.

With 1,320 passengers aboard, *Liberté* was scheduled to sail on her maiden crossing from Le Havre at four o'clock in the afternoon on 17 August. A sudden dispute between the ship's engineers and the French Line developed and caused a six-hour delay. Then there was a further two-hour hold-up at Southampton. There was no delay in her scheduled arrival in New York, however. There were still 100 workers aboard for the crossing, adding the finishing touches. One passenger noted: 'We grew accustomed to seeing women sewing carpeting in the public rooms.'

A New York journalist, Naomi Jolles Barry, was aboard that maiden westbound crossing:

Three and a half years of work have taken all the German atmosphere out of the old *Europa* and transformed her into a completely French ship. She has the same feeling of unweighted luxury that characterized the *Normandie*, whose memory is still cherished proudly by the French. Among the *Liberté's* personnel, many of whom served on the *Normandie*, there is a general feeling that at last the days of grandeur have returned. There is even a physical link with the past. The large, gilded bronze plaque that decorates the *Liberté's* first class Smoking Room comes from the Smoking Room of the *Normandie*. During her long refit at St Nazaire, a new liner was born.

Ms Barry continued:

The sombre mahogany, walnut and ebony interior was replaced with pale woods – Norwegian and Canadian birch, cherry wood, ash and sycamore. The old subdued illumination was succeeded by fixtures that blaze with light. One of the most charming rooms … is the Cabin Class Children's Dining Room where murals depict the Feast of Sleeping Beauty. Among other interesting features of this ship is a small music room, which opens off to the vast First Class Salon. It is for musician passengers who want to practice unobtrusively on their crossing.

Maiden voyage: the splendid-looking *Liberté* leaves Le Havre on 17 August 1950. (Cronican-Arroyo Collection)

Artist Don Stoltenberg's depiction of *Île de France* in the 1930s. (Don Stoltenberg Collection)

Île de France at Le Havre in 1955. (French Line)

LA CIGOGNE

De Grasse in a wintery Hudson River in 1949. (Author's Collection)

During a tugboat strike, the great Île de France carefully berths 'unassisted' at Pier 88, 15 February 1957. (Allen Pellymounter Collection)

Île de France departs from New York. (Author's Collection)

Île de France arrives at New York's Pier 88. (Allen Pellymounter Collection)

Against the Lower Manhattan skyline, Île de France makes a late afternoon departure from New York. (Author's Collection)

Île de France at sea in the western Atlantic. (Richard Faber Collection)

A painting of the *Île* at Le Havre by artist P. Bortolozzi. (Author's Collection)

Île de France departs from New York on a summer's day. (Author's Collection)

The sitting room of the Chantilly Suite aboard *Île de France*. (Author's Collection)

Île de France anchored off Plymouth. (Allen Pellymounter Collection)

Printed memorabilia from *Île de France*.
(Brian Hawley Collection)

Additional collectibles from *Île de France*.
(Brian Hawley Collection)

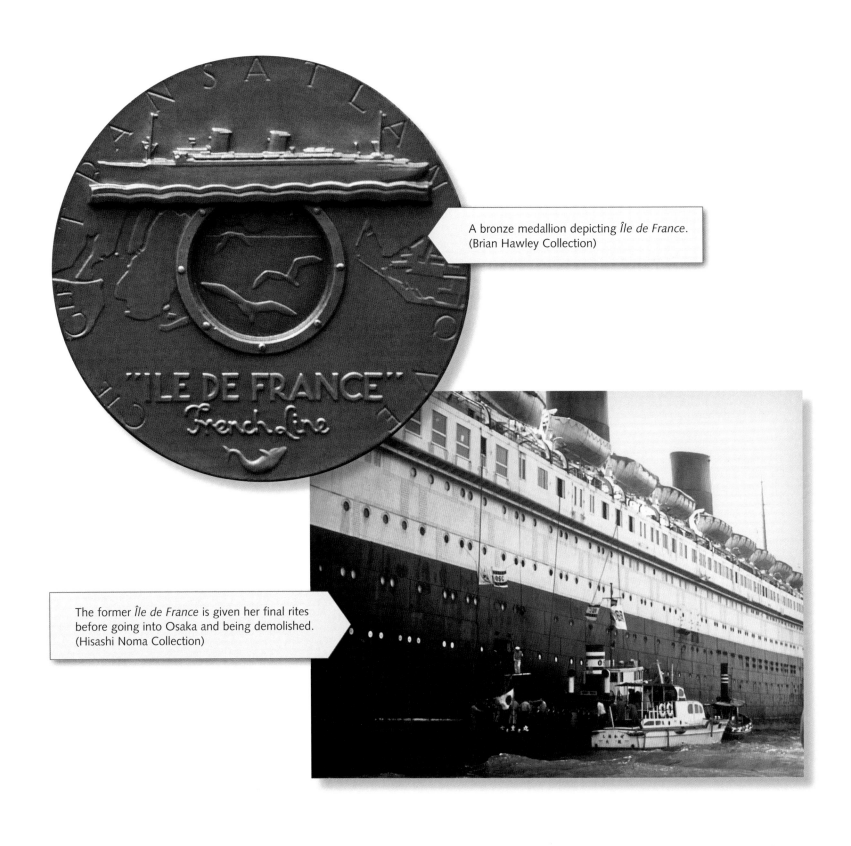

A bronze medallion depicting *Île de France*.
(Brian Hawley Collection)

The former *Île de France* is given her final rites before going into Osaka and being demolished.
(Hisashi Noma Collection)

Liberté arrives at Le Havre following her post-war refit. (Luis Miguel Correia Collection)

Liberté approaches New York Harbour. (Gillespie-Faber Collection)

A fine painting of *Liberté* while berthed at Le Havre. (Author's Collection)

A popular poster depicting *Liberté*. (Author's Collection)

Albert Brenet was one of the greatest marine artists and he created this poster for the French Line in 1953. (Author's Collection)

Liberté was indeed the great Atlantic liner. (Author's Collection)

Liberté berthed at Pier 88, New York. (Author's Collection)

Outbound from New York on a summer's day. (Author's Collection)

Another fine view of the 936ft-long *Liberté* at New York. (Luis Miguel Correia Collection)

Liberté departs from Le Havre with *Île de France* behind. (Philippe Brebant Collection)

An advertisement for the French Line from September 1953. (National Geographic Society)

Artist P. Bortoluzzi created this fine rendition of *Liberté* at her Le Havre berth. (Author's Collection)

The Arosa Line's *Arosa Sky*, the former French *La Marseillaise*, is berthed on the opposite side of Pier 88 from *Liberté* in this view from 1957. (Author's Collection)

The towering aft funnel of *Liberté*.
(Philippe Brebant Collection)

The final departure from New York of *Liberté*
in November 1961. (Author's Collection)

De Grasse, ex-*Bergensfjord*, at sea in the Caribbean. (Philippe Brebant Collection)

The giant *France* in the graving dock at Le Havre. (Fred Rodriguez Collection)

New York maritime reporter Walter Hamshar also reported from the gala crossing:

> With over 1,300 excited and critical passengers to watch her first performance, France's largest, fastest and possibly most luxurious liner, the *Liberté*, has opened up on the great stage of the Atlantic. A liner's maiden voyage is like an opening night at the theatre – stewards, more than one to every two passengers, nervous and uncertain; the cabins like stage props somewhat unfinished; the departure like a curtain that is probably late; no critic is more demanding than a first class passenger.

He continued:

> Aboard the *Liberté*, one is isolated from the ocean as in a walled French estate. From chapel to swimming pool, from movie theatre to smoking room and bar, there is only an accidental glimpse of the Atlantic. Headwinds and squalls have ruffled the summer seas, but not the passengers who visit the boutiques, the florist shop, the coiffeur or the Cafe de L'Atlantique up on the Sun Deck. It's a shakedown cruise and anything is liable to happen. Some of the usual service problems have happened already. But most of those who bought passage, including almost 300 stranded by an accident to the *Île de France*, are willing to pay the price of some inconvenience for the gala maiden voyage on this new flagship of the French Line.

June Jones was aboard the maiden crossing and had somewhat different impressions:

> The ship was pushed into service a month early. There was great demand for passages, especially to be home for the Jewish holy days. The boat train from Paris up to Le Havre was overcrowded. There were summer storms in France which caused delays with the boat train. The ship was waiting. Jack Carter [a well-known American comedian] was sailing as well. The suite page boys were waiting at the terminal. It looked like a Philip Morris convention. After boarding, I later went to the dining room, but soon felt seasick. I left the table, went to the open deck and soon realised we were still at the pier! On the crossing, the ship's brand new lighting was too pale. In the dining room, it turned the meat a grey colour and made passengers seasick. The lighting was changed at New York. We lost all fresh water on the first day out. There was not enough

Greatly enhancing the French Line's service to and from New York, *Liberté* approaches New York Harbour on 23 August 1950. (Moran Towing & Transportation Co.)

There are couches and chairs for invited guests and a Gaveau baby grand piano made in Norwegian birch to harmonize with the furniture. An idea also used on the *Normandie* is a Winter Garden, arranged as a conservatory with exotic plants and flowers. The library, an imposing two decks in height, contains 5,000 specially bound volumes. But the centre of fun on this boat is destined to be the Cafe de l'Atlantique, the night club high up on the Sun Deck and where the dance floor is illuminated from beneath by coloured electric bulbs.

Looking every inch the great and grand liner, *Liberté* is inbound along the Hudson River, just opposite West 25th Street. (Moran Towing & Transportation Co.)

Tugs move *Liberté* into her berth, the north side of Pier 88 at the foot of West 48th Street. The stern of Cunard's *Caronia* is on the left, while an American Export Lines freighter and the Italian liner *Conte Biancamano* are top right. (Moran Towing & Transportation Co.)

bottled water so we used champagne for the basics and saltwater for bathing. But then there was not enough saltwater soap. Maiden voyages can be difficult. You need a sense of humour!

Liberté arrived in New York late on Wednesday afternoon, 23 August. That same day eight other passenger ships arrived as well: *Veendam*, *Brasil*, *Santa Rosa*, *Stratheden*, *Queen of Bermuda*, *Fort Amherst*, *Fort Townshend* and *Cristobal*. She remained at Pier 88 for only two nights, sailing late on Friday afternoon and, while off West 35th Street, passed the inbound *Île de France* (with 968 passengers aboard).

A small army of New York reporters greeted *Liberté*. They asked of the ship, her performance and of the future. The French Line officials said, however, that no big liners were planned as they were 'studying developments with air travel' and then they were asked about reports that pipes had burst during the crossing and some passengers had to make do

with limited water. The purser reportedly smiled, and responded: 'After all, we are French. The passengers could bathe in Champagne!'

A month after her maiden voyage, *Liberté* was back in the news. She was caught in the eye of a hurricane off the New England coast, lashed by 100mph winds and giant waves that were seven decks above sea level in height. An American ambassador was aboard and later commented: 'I boarded the ship to criticize and I leave with nothing but praise.' A week later she ran into an obstruction at Southampton, but was freed within four hours. Five tugs had been sent to the liner's aid.

Liberté took a break from Atlantic crossings and on 11 February 1952 set off on a twenty-eight-day cruise to the Caribbean and South America. Reminiscent of *Normandie*'s two Carnival-in-Rio cruises in February 1938 and February 1939, *Liberté* retraced something of her itinerary, calling at Martinique, Barbados and Bahia, then four days in Rio de Janeiro, before returning via Trinidad and Nassau. The minimum

Liberté moves into her berth, with *Caronia* on the left and the little French Line freighter *Bresle* on the right. (Moran Towing & Transportation Co.)

Outbound in the afternoon of 25 August 1950, *Liberté* passes her running mate, *Île de France*. (Moran Towing & Transportation Co.)

fare was $925. Some thirty additional staff joined the cruise to assist the 731 passengers who altogether paid a total of $1.2 million in fares. Only first-class and some cabin-class cabins were used, and passengers had the full run of the ship.

There was further proof of the atmosphere of style, elegance and gaiety, all difficult to define precisely, that is incipient in all French ships. The *Liberté* was certainly no exception. With over 100 crossings begun in 1937, Lewis and Ruth Gordon preferred the French Line above all others and thought of *Liberté* as one of their favourite ships:

The *Liberté* had the most magnificent stairway in first class. Passengers, especially the ladies, could make the *grand descent*. We could watch, looking at all the superb clothes especially just before and after dinner. The *Liberté* always seemed to have a great number of passengers from the theatrical world. I remember Elizabeth Taylor & Mike Todd on one

trip [1958]. The food was absolutely superb such as Skate in butter sauce for breakfast and skyscraper-thick Filet Mignon and there were 2 bottles of complimentary wine at every table. Of course, like most Atlantic liners back then, there was no entertainment. Mostly, we sat around for 5 or 6 days.

Reverend Neville Rucker recalled *Liberté* from a 1959 crossing:

The grand staircase was the big thing on board. It had grandeur, which so suited that great ocean liner. She was truly a grand dame of the seas! But we hit a terrible storm. All the passengers were sent to bed or so it seemed. We had 12 or 13 hours of torturous weather. The ship, even as large as she was, was lifting out of the water. But the four props kept churning. The ship was shuddering. It was quite frightening. There were lots of broken arms, even among the crew.

There were the periodic strikes, disruptions and unexpected delays. She was laid up during one strike in May 1953, for example. On 8 September 1953, she went aground in fog at Le Havre. Later towed off the sandbar by six tugs, there was no significant damage. Another French liner, *De Grasse*, had gone aground at exactly the same point in 1950 and was refloated after six hours without damage. On 2 October 1953, in the early morning darkness, *Liberté* cautiously berthed herself at Pier 88 during a New York Harbour tugboat strike. Then, in January 1954, there was a fire in a storeroom on board while she lay at her Le Havre berth. In February 1955, in a bitterly cold winter, *Liberté* arrived at Pier 88 but had to make three attempts to dock in the ice-choked Hudson. On 29 December 1956, the New York-bound ship was forced to turn back to Le Havre because of bad weather in the mid-Atlantic. With 533 passengers aboard, the violent storm had smashed three cargo booms and stoved in a cargo hatch. Another strike erupted at the peak of the summer season in June 1957, and sailings were cancelled for the 1,405 passengers on *Liberté* and the 1,228 on *Île de France*.

Just before daybreak on 1 October 1953, *Liberté* arrives without the assistance of tugs. There is a strike and so the giant liner must very carefully berth herself, a process that takes over two hours. (Cronican-Arroyo Collection)

Four liners at Le Havre – from left to right: *Liberté*, *United States*, *Île de France* and *Antilles*. (Author's Collection)

Late afternoon at Le Havre, with *Liberté* in the centre and *Île de France* in the far-right distance. (Author's Collection)

'On February 10th 1956, the *Liberté* sailed from Le Havre, fully loaded with passengers, but soon developed some sort of engine trouble,' recalled Philippe Brebant. 'She had to reverse course and offload all her passengers. Their plans were completely disrupted, being sent to hotels in and around Le Havre, and then re-booked on other ships. The *Liberté* herself had to go to dry dock at Le Havre and miss a roundtrip.'

Increasingly, the French had to look to the future. In November 1953, the first rumours began in New York that the French were considering a replacement for both *Liberté* and *Île de France*. Two types of ship were being considered: a 50–60,000-ton vessel with a service speed of over 30 knots; and a 30–40,000-ton ship capable of 27 knots. In March 1955, it was said that a 58,000-ton liner would be built and 'almost certainly named the *France*'.

'The first thought toward building a new liner, a big liner in fact, for French Line Atlantic service actually began in 1949,' reported Philippe Brebant:

But there were political problems in the way & so the project dragged on. French Line had planned to have such a new liner in service by 1955, but everything moved very slowly. Consequently, construction on the ship that became the *France* did not begin until September 1957. And so she was seven years late, you might say, arriving for the first time in 1962. It really was too late, in ways, considering that jet travel on the Atlantic began in 1958, over three years before the maiden voyage of the *France* …

For a time, French Line thought of building two new replacement ships. Preliminary thoughts ranged from 30,000 to 50,000 tons for each ship. The crews of the *Liberté* and *Île de France* much preferred the two-ship idea. This would guarantee further employment for the crews of each older ship …

There was also thought given to converting the two basically Caribbean liners, the *Flandre* & *Antilles*, for improved transatlantic service. Then, in 1957, there was a plan to convert the large, 30,000-ton *Pasteur*, then used as a French troopship but soon being decommissioned, for luxury service to New York. But there were political problems, namely French shipyards wanting to build a large, brand new ship and thereby employing many more French shipyard workers. A Government evaluation of converting the *Pasteur* was actually rigged. It stated that the *Pasteur* was 'not suited' to North Atlantic service. Well, of course, she was later sold to the Germans, superbly rebuilt as the *Bremen* and used in very successful Atlantic sailings. Clearly, the *Pasteur* could have been converted.

Peter Fialkowski recalled *Liberté*:

My memories of the *Liberté* are far clearer than my trip on the *Île de France*, as that crossing from New York was six years later, on a drab overcast June 14th 1960. By then I fancied myself something of a veteran, having also sailed on the all-but-ancient *Franconia* to Quebec City and the newer *Ivernia* to Montreal. Our cabin on the *Liberté* was #159 on Main deck, past a fire door that didn't close properly and to the end of the corridor.

These days cruise ships offer rather feeble water pressure in the bath tubs or showers. That was not the case on the *Liberté*! The bathtub faucet was a very large rectangular affair, and when the taps were turned, it would produce a thunderous Niagara that could fill the tub in one minute! I can't imagine why the ship didn't run out of fresh water when a large number of passengers were bathing.

Speaking of fresh water, one had a choice of salt or fresh water with four taps. Of course, I had to see what would happen if all four taps were open at the same time. Oddly enough, it was the fresh water that won the battle and the salt water would be shut off. The toilet, by the way, used salt water, which was, of course in the days way before the modern-day vacuum systems, explosively powerful!

While awaiting the departure, we strolled around the deck. Then stepping inside from the enclosed promenade deck, we found ourselves in a gallery with some shop windows and, up a few steps, the cinema. But when I turned around, I was confronted with the most impressive vista of public rooms I have ever seen on a ship, better even than today's *Queen Mary 2*. The vista went right down through the centre of the library, through the grand salon, two galleries and on to the smoking room. It puzzled me why I never encountered such an impressive vista of public rooms on ships I subsequently travelled on, including *Queen Elizabeth*, *QE2* and the *France*. Eventually, of course, I found out about split uptakes to the funnels.

The beauty of travelling on first class, as we spoilt youngsters did back in 1960, was that we shared the ship's most impressive public rooms only with fellow first class passengers. Everyone else was crammed in cabin and tourist class at the stern and bow of the ship. These days on the *Queen Mary 2*, there are one or two public areas exclusively for grill passengers, but for the most part in these democratic times, they have to share the major public rooms with everyone else. Not so, on the *Liberté*!

The main lounge or Grand Salon was vast with high ceilings and was lavishly decorated. The CGT staff would spoil us youngsters rotten, and my sister and I would spend hours playing checkers on a sofa at the corner of the lounge beneath golden lacquered bas relief panels of a hunting scene created in a typical 1930s style. These were installed around the large glass exit doors that led to the library. At that age I had never heard of the *Normandie* and didn't realise that I was seated below the Jean Dunand panels from that ship. What a thrill it was to rediscover some of those panels many years later in the *Normandie* Restaurant onboard *Celebrity Summit*, currently one of my favourite ships.

Just behind us and at right angles to the panels was the *Salle Lafayette* or music room. At the age of nine, my sister, who is now an international concert pianist, was already immersed in practising the piano. The *Salle Lafayette* offered the perfect environment, handsomely decorated in a sort of post-war art deco with a matching baby grand piano (that I occasionally got to play) all under the watchful eye of Lafayette himself in a painting at the foot of the room. The ceilings of the room were quite high as were the doors, which, by the way, could be locked from the inside to prevent interruptions from other passengers. (The *France* had a similar but low-ceilinged room just outside the cinema, but this offered no lock on the door, and interruptions were frequent.)

During tea time in the afternoon the largest string orchestra I have experienced on a ship would entertain the passengers. This included two violinists, a cellist, a double bass, drums and a huge concert grand piano. But we didn't tarry for long for tea in the lounge, as we had to hurry to

The magnificent grand salon in first class aboard *Liberté*. (French Line)

The Cafe de l'Atlantique, also in first class aboard *Liberté*. (French Line)

The first-class library. (French Line)

The first-class smoking room. (French Line)

The reading and writing room, also in first class. (French Line)

The main salon in tourist class. (French Line)

The main foyer. (French Line)

The first-class dining room. (French Line)

the cinema for the day's movie. The films would alternate between French and English language.

After dinner, the stewards would roll up the large carpet for the evening's dancing, which sadly I was too young to attend.

Upon leaving the main lounge, we would pass through a wide passageway or gallery, which, in marked contrast to the rest of the ship, was panelled in rather tired looking wood and which vibrated noisily. In fact there was a constant rumbling sound in the area coupled with a warm stuffy atmosphere. Years later, while looking at the deck plans, I realised this was where the passageway went between the split uptakes.

The finest walk around promenade deck I have ever experienced is on the *Queen Mary 2*, but one managed pretty well on the *Liberté*. Sure one had to pass through 'cabin class only' barriers, but even if these were closed, and often they weren't, all one had to do is unlatch the barrier and walk through. We were never challenged. Then down and back up a couple of stairways at the stern and back one would come on the other side of the ship. Mind you, there was no wind protection where the deck rounded the bridge and one had to make every effort not to be swept off one's feet!

Deck tennis was on the games deck high up between the funnels. Now I had already been impressed by the *Île de France*'s two huge and rather modernistic funnels, and while the *Franconia*'s old-fashioned stove-pipe

The sitting room adjoins the bedroom of the Algerie Suite. (French Line)

An outside double in first class, a room priced from $600 in high season for the six days to Southampton and Le Havre in the mid-1950s. (French Line)

funnel was very tall, but the *Liberté*'s two funnels were enormous. I was aware that the *Liberté* had once been the German *Europa*, but didn't know how low the funnels had been in the early 1930s. I could, however, clearly see a seam half way up the funnels where I now realise the extensions were added.

Throughout our crossing the seas remained calm, though one day while crossing the Gulf Stream we did encounter fog. Oddly enough I never heard the *Liberté*'s whistle, though I well remembered the thunderous blast of the whistles on the *Île*, *Franconia* and *Ivernia*. During that day in the fog, the *Liberté* sounded a sort of 'woop – woop – woop' fog horn in ascending notes, that one usually associates with warships.

The weather may have been pleasant for deck sports or walks, but it was too chilly for lounging on a deck chair. For that we joined our fellow first class passengers in the enclosed promenade deck. Unlike Cunarders, which had teak decks, the *Liberté*'s enclosed promenade deck featured a rubberised surface, terra cotta in colour, and embossed with small squares. Whether immersed in a book or dozing, we would be aroused at around 11am by the rumbling sound of the cart carrying hot bouillon as it was pushed along the rough surface. By the way that surface must have been a success as it was installed on the *France* two years later, although the colour was a light grey.

The lavish sitting room of the Normandie Suite. (Cronican-Arroyo Collection)

The sitting room of the Alsace Suite. (Cronican-Arroyo Collection)

Another view of the sitting room of the Alsace Suite. (Cronican-Arroyo Collection)

The chapel aboard *Liberté*. (Cronican-Arroyo Collection)

The cinema aboard *Liberté*. (French Line)

The beautiful indoor pool. (French Line)

The first-class children's playroom. (French Line)

The cabin-class playroom. (Cronican-Arroyo Collection)

During that wonderful crossing in June, the main topic of conversation amongst the crew members was the soon to be completed *France*. Two years later, the *Liberté* was but a memory, and we boarded the brand new French flagship at Le Havre only to find many familiar faces amongst the crew. When we mentioned to our dining room steward, maitre d'hotel, sommelier and chief deck steward that we recognised them from the *Liberté*, they proudly replied 'Yes, and before that I served for many years on the *Île*!' Although after the war the *Liberté* was the more luxurious of the two ships, it was obvious that the *Île de France* remained the sentimental favourite, rather than the former German liner.

For us, the stark but luxurious and high quality modernity of the interiors of the *France* temporarily dazzled us. However, when we returned to that ship in 1966, it was obvious that things had changed: the era of the loud and crass passenger had begun! Now, many years later, it is the old *Liberté* that I remember most fondly.

In July 1959, the former French *Pasteur* as the luxurious German *Bremen* arrived in New York for the first time. George Horne, maritime editor for the *New York Times*, took note of the occasion:

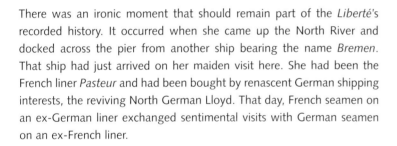

Liberté outbound in Southampton Water. (French Line)

Approaching Le Havre. (Philippe Brebant Collection)

There was an ironic moment that should remain part of the *Liberté*'s recorded history. It occurred when she came up the North River and docked across the pier from another ship bearing the name *Bremen*. That ship had just arrived on her maiden visit here. She had been the French liner *Pasteur* and had been bought by renascent German shipping interests, the reviving North German Lloyd. That day, French seamen on an ex-German liner exchanged sentimental visits with German seamen on an ex-French liner.

While the jets had begun flying over the Atlantic just nine months before, in October 1958, and the 'great shift' away from traditional liners had started, there was still some deep faith and optimism in the future by steamship lines. Two months after *Bremen*, the Dutch added *Rotterdam*. Italy's *Leonardo da Vinci* was commissioned the following summer. And of course the biggest of all, *France*, was due to emerge in the winter of 1962. But time was running out for the 'old guard': the veteran, ageing Atlantic liners. After *Île de France* was withdrawn in the autumn of 1958, *Liberté* operated alongside the smaller *Flandre* for the next three years; in winter, when *Flandre* shifted to West Indies service, *Liberté* was alone.

On a summery afternoon in June 1960, one of the last great gatherings of ocean liners along Manhattan's West Side piers, the famed 'Luxury Liner Row', occurred. *Liberté* was among the eight ships, but almost as something of a 'grandmother'. Of the same age, dating from 1930, Cunard's *Britannic* was included, but was actually laid up with a seriously broken crankshaft. Obviously, there was little interest in repairing such a veteran ship. She went to the breakers that December. *Liberté* would be next it seemed. She made her final round-trip crossing from Le Havre on 2 November 1961. Some 1,050 passengers were aboard that last westbound crossing.

Beginning months before, rumours circulated as to her fate. One proposal, from a Luxembourg-based firm, hinted that she might become a floating medical research centre. Another would see her become a floating casino moored off the California coast. Then the scrappers, including the Japanese, were interested, of course. But there was another, more persistent idea: using the ship as a moored hotel for the 1962 World's Fair at Seattle. With a shortage of hotel rooms, she would join two other hotel ships: Mexico's *Acapulco* and Britain's *Dominion Monarch*. The French Line were in favour of the plan, which would see *Liberté* having restaurants with French food, shops with French goods and clubs with French entertainment. She would be highlighted as a 'floating French city'. Afterwards, as projected to both the Seattle interests (Northwest Leasing Corporation) and the French Line itself, the liner would sail to Japan for scrapping.

Seen at New York's Pier 88 on her penultimate visit, 19 October 1961. (Gillespie-Faber Collection)

Arriving at Le Havre. (Philippe Brebant Collection)

A superb view of *Liberté* at sea, hitting some 23 knots during one of her normal Atlantic crossings. (Author's Collection)

Another superb view: a sketch by noted artist Carl Evers of *Liberté* being berthed at Pier 88, which was created for the October 1955 cover of *Towline*, the monthly journal of Moran Towing & Transportation Co. (Moran Towing & Transportation Co.)

Liberté approaches Le Havre. (Luis Miguel Correia Collection)

The stern of *Liberté* just prior to departure from Pier 88 in February 1959. (Author's Collection)

Heavy weather: a great wave covers the foredeck of *Liberté* during a westbound crossing in 1957. (Richard Faber Collection)

Preparing to sail: *Liberté* at Le Havre. (Author's Collection)

A handsome view but actually her final arrival at Le Havre in November 1961. (Luis Miguel Correia Collection)

New York maritime journalist George Horne mourned the passing of *Liberté*:

Not many great ships have had three careers under three flags. Such has been the case, however, with the *Liberté*, whose final career is now ending. And so, when she stands out to sea from the Port of New York for the last time next Friday, fireboat salutes and deep-throated harbor whistles will record a warm farewell for a superb old liner. The French Line in a few months will bring out its new 66,000-ton *France*, and the 51,000-ton *Liberté* has been consigned to the scrap heap. Her vast public rooms – the grand salon is called the largest of any ship in the world – are still elegant and gay in the French manner. Her staterooms, mostly with Old World spaciousness that is uncommon in modern ship design, are still popular with her travelers; her cooking is for gourmets. And to the viewer as she moves downriver and out to sea, she unquestionably presents an aspect of grandeur as of old. But she thirsts for oil, and is too expensive to meet the competition of newer and more efficient vessels …

Obsolete the *Liberté* may be, but she has a following. Bob Hope, who traveled on one of her recent passages, has offered to buy the liner's beautiful chapel, marble altar and all. Others have bid on some furnishings. A man from Texas sent a laconic note that he is interested

Bon voyage! *Liberté* poetically heads off for Southampton and then across to New York. (Author's Collection)

Liners passing: the inbound *Liberté* passes the outbound *Mauretania* in this aerial view dated 25 January 1957. (Moran Towing & Transportation Co.)

Liberté approaches New York with the newly fitted domes on her funnels, 13 May 1954. (French Line)

Through a cargo loading door, *Liberté* is captured by Jeff Blinn, Moran Towing's skilled harbour photographer. (Moran Towing & Transportation Co.)

Luxury Liner Row at New York: *Liberté* was included in the largest gathering of liners in Manhattan since 1939. The date is 9 July 1958 and from top to bottom are: *Vulcania*, *Constitution*, *America*, *United States*, *Liberté*, *Mauretania*, *Queen Elizabeth* and *Britannic*. (Port Authority of New York & New Jersey)

After making a late morning departure, the classic *Liberté* outbound off the tip of Lower Manhattan. (Richard Faber Collection)

End of the line: *Liberté* departs from New York for the last time on 10 November 1961. (Moran Towing & Transportation Co.)

in buying outmoded liners. He wanted her, he wrote, fully equipped and planned to keep her in a preserved state, never to go to sea again.

The autumn day 10 November 1961 was superb at New York: with a clear, bright sun and a slight chill in the air. The seasonal leaves had begun to fall, the days were shorter and there was the sense of winter on the horizon. That morning, at Pier 88, *Liberté* was preparing for a special voyage: her final crossing to Southampton and Le Havre, and, more so, her final voyage with fare-paying passengers. She was near the end of her thirty-one-year career. Smoke drifted upwards from her twin funnels as baggage and the final stores were loaded aboard and passengers embarked. Some had booked the otherwise late season crossing to Europe for the sentimental reason of making this last voyage on the famed ship. It was, in fact, the end for two ships – her early days as *Europa* and now as *Liberté*. It had been a long, diverse and largely illustrious career. Some might have remembered her as well from her short phase as USS *Europa*, from her trooping voyages at the end of the Second World War.

'The pomp and pageantry usually reserved to incoming ship royalty was accorded to the *Liberté*, the retiring queen of the French merchant marine, as the graceful old liner headed out of port for the last time yesterday afternoon,' reported maritime editor Werner Bamberger in the *New York Times* on 11 November. 'The liner sailed into shipping history through a mantle of rainbows created by sunlight streaming through cascades of water from two city fireboats. During her slow passage down the Hudson River, the vessel exchanged deep-throated "adieus" with ferries, harbor craft and ocean liners, among them Holland America's *Rotterdam*, which followed her out to sea.' According to waterfront observers, the farewell given to *Liberté* was a better send-off than some new vessels had received here on their maiden arrivals. A fire department member added: 'As a rule only one fireboat is called out to greet incoming vessels.'

Days later, in a bank office in Jersey City, a deal was signed in which *Liberté* was sold to Northwest Leasing for $3.1 million. Singer Bing Crosby was said to be one of the officers of the Seattle-based firm. The ship itself would be transferred in January and afterwards be towed through the

Panama Canal to Seattle for use as a hotel. She was to be moored at a pier 2 miles from downtown Seattle and some French Line seamen might be hired to maintain the ship. Northwest officials were enthusiastic and indicated that the liner might be moved to other American ports, including a return to New York for the 1964–65 World's Fair. However, within little more than a month there were complications, namely financial problems on the part of Northwest. On 27 December, the French Line suggested that other American as well as Italian and Yugoslavian firms had shown an interest in the ship, but for restricted, non-sailing purposes. Two days later, the Italians won – *Liberté* was sold to scrappers for $2.2 million. In

New York, the buyers were identified as the India Trading & Transport Association and Luria Brothers & Company. Briefly in January, and while the liner was idle and waiting at Le Havre, rumours resurfaced that the Seattle hotel ship project was still a possibility, but nothing came to pass. A small crew delivered *Liberté* to La Spezia for scrapping. On 26 January, the brand-new *France*, while returning from her inaugural cruise to the Canary Islands, paid tribute to the former French flagship. The two liners crossed in the Atlantic, off St Nazaire, and exchanged whistle salutes. By that summer, *Liberté* was completely demolished.

Laid up and awaiting a final sale to Italian scrappers, *Liberté* is at dock at Le Havre as the brand-new *France* returns from an inaugural cruise to the Canary Islands. (French Line)

TO THE WEST INDIES: *COLOMBIE*

'After the War, throughout the 1950s, *Colombie* had a very high reputation within France for food, for service and for her drinks, especially rum drinks,' noted Philippe Brebant. 'She had a loyal following, but then grew older and showed signs of age.'

Built in 1931 purposely for the Le Havre–Southampton/Plymouth–West Indies service, this 13,300grt, white-hulled liner was seized by the Americans at Casablanca just after the attack on Pearl Harbor in December 1941. Used as a troopship (with a full capacity for 2,683 against her

1931-

The 1931-built *Colombie* was rebuilt after the Second World War with a single tapered, more modern funnel. She served the French Line for over thirty years. (Cronican-Arroyo Collection)

The former *Colombie* in the Typaldos Lines' colours as the *Atlantica* in a view from 1964. (Alex Duncan)

peacetime maximum of 491), the 508ft-long ship was converted in 1945 to the hospital ship *Aleda E Lutz*. She was fitted with quarters for as many as 828 patients. A year later, in April 1946, she was decommissioned and formally returned to the French Line at New York's Pier 88.

After a thorough and modernising refit (her twin funnels were replaced by one of a far more modern design), her passenger accommodations were upgraded as well and with 192 first class, 140 cabin class and 246 tourist class. She resumed sailings, being partnered mostly with the brand-new, 20,000grt *Antilles*, to the West Indies – to Guadeloupe

and Martinique as well as St Lucia, Trinidad and Barbados. The 16-knot *Colombie* also ran occasional cruises from Le Havre. At 33 years of age, in 1964 she was sold to Greek buyers, the Typaldos Lines, and renamed *Atlantica* for Mediterranean cruising. A charter might have brought her to New York in 1965, as *Atlantic II*, but it never materialised. When Typaldos collapsed in 1967, the aged *Atlantica* was laid up before being partially scrapped in 1970; her remaining hull was towed to Barcelona in 1974 for final demolition.

6

FRENCH TWINS: *FLANDRE & ANTILLES*

While spending was a serious consideration, air travel was looming in the distant future as a threat and so the French Line did not build big, lavish liners in the early 1950s, but instead ordered a pair of rather moderate, intermediate liners in 1950 for their Le Havre–West Indies trade. But as the first of these, *Flandre*, was nearing completion at Dunkirk, there was a change in plan. She would go on the New York service, at least for two-thirds of the year, and replace the aged *De Grasse*. The second ship, *Antilles*, constructed at Brest, would remain as planned for Caribbean service, joining the 1931-built *Colombie* and a reassigned *De Grasse*. 'They were sometimes called the "black & white sisters",' noted Philippe Brebant. 'Of course, in the beginning, the *Flandre* had a black hull while the *Antilles* had a white one.'

Brebant added:

> Both the *Flandre* & *Antilles* were specially designed for the Atlantic, for rough weather, and so had huge bows. They were almost like battleships. They were first designed to be larger, at about 650 feet in length, but in a cost reduction were completed at 600 feet. If they had been larger as first designed, they would have most likely been rebuilt as replacements for the *Île de France* and the *Liberté*. Simply, there would not have been a *France* of 1962. From the start, the two new ships were to be replacement 'cabin liners,' as they were called, for the pre-war *Lafayette* and *Champlain*. The *Flandre* & *Antilles* were also designed with the tropics in mind, for winter sailings to the Caribbean, especially Martinique & Guadeloupe. In the beginning, they had only partial air-conditioning, however, but were fitted with an outdoor swimming pool …

The brand-new *Flandre* at New York's Pier 88 in July 1952. (Cronican-Arroyo Collection)

Both ships were known as 'great rollers' when at sea. They were not especially good 'sea boats'. They were different than the larger liners, the *Île de France* and the *Liberté*, and later the *France*. They were smaller, more intimate ships. The larger liners were completely different, with a different ambience. The crews liked them because onboard they were like small families. Their crews felt close.

On her maiden trip to New York in July 1952, the 20,469grt, 784-passenger *Flandre* broke down. She even had to be towed into New York for her inaugural reception. Afterwards, the 22-knot ship was returned to her builders for nine months of repairs. 'The *Antilles* was delayed [until January 1953] because of last-minute changes in her construction,' reported Philippe Brebant. 'These were a result of the earlier problems with the *Flandre*.'

Flandre was sold off in 1968, becoming the rebuilt cruise ship *Carla C* and later *Carla Costa* for Italy's Costa Cruises. In 1992 she was sold to Greek owners, the Epirotiki Lines, and became *Pallas Athena*. She was destroyed by fire at Piraeus on 23 March 1994 and her scorched remains were scrapped in Turkey in 1995. *Antilles* also burned and was destroyed. Off the Caribbean island of Mustique, she caught fire on 8 January 1971, then began to sink and broke in two and finally three pieces.

A late morning departure as a Moran tug assists the 600ft-long *Flandre*. (Moran Towing & Transportation Co.)

The all-white *Antilles* serviced the Caribbean. (French Line)

CRUISING FRENCH STYLE: THE *DE GRASSE* OF 1956

To replace the fire-gutted *Antilles* in 1971, the French Line hurriedly bought the 18,500grt, 1956-built *Bergensfjord* from the Norwegian America Line and refitted her as the cruise ship *De Grasse*. 'Buying the *Bergensfjord* from the Norwegians was only as a quick replacement for the *Antilles*,' reported Philippe Brebant:

Before the fire [in January 1971], Costa wanted to buy the *Antilles* and have her join her sister, the former *Flandre*, then already sailing for Costa as the *Carla C*. But Costa had many mechanical problems with the former *Flandre* and so lost interest. But still, the French Line wanted to sell the *Antilles*. The fire was a great mystery. There were many rumours in France that the fire was actually 'sabotage'. Afterwards, of course, the Government inquiry was completed and classified the loss of the ship as an 'accident' …

Purchasing the *Bergensfjord* was also merely to appease the French unions. The French, it was said, even over-paid for the ship.

The 577ft-long ship, originally to have been renamed *Louisiane*, lasted for only two years under the French flag before being sold to Norwegian buyers, who renamed her *Rasa Sayang* (Flower of the East) for Southeast Asian cruising from Singapore. This new phase ended quite quickly, however, as she caught fire while at sea on 6 June 1977. Adrift for some time, she was later taken in tow and subsequently repaired, but her reputation in travel circles had been seriously damaged. Sold in June 1978 to Greek interests, she became *Golden Moon*, presumably for Mediterranean cruising. This never came to pass and instead the 18,739grt ship was to go on charter to the Dutch as *Prins van Oranje*. However, this too failed to materialise. Finally, the London-based CTC Line was to restore her as *Rasa Sayang*, but for Australian-based cruising. Unfortunately, on 27 August 1980, while undergoing repairs at Piraeus, Greece, she was swept by fire. Her charred hull was towed to outer harbour waters and then deliberately sunk.

OTHER LINERS UNDER THE TRICOLOUR

'There was considerable political pressure in the 1950s to build new passenger ships, including ones for the French Line's service to North Africa & to Casablanca,' noted Philippe Brebant.

In 1960, with *Liberté* operating on the North Atlantic with the smaller *Flandre*, and with the French Line awaiting the brand-new *France* due in 1962, the company's Caribbean service was looked after by *Antilles* and the ageing *Colombie*. However, the company's passenger ship fleet was not restricted to the Atlantic. Serving North and West Africa as well as Corsica were the 10,000grt sisters *Ville D'Alger* and *Ville D'Oran*, as well as *Ville de Marseilles*, *Ville de Tunis*, *Ville de Bordeaux*, *Napoleon*, *Charles Plumier*, *Gouverneur General Chanzy*, *Commandant Quere* and *Sampiero Corso*. Messageries Maritimes was second in size for French passenger ships and tended to service colonial or former colonial ports. There were three splendid combination passenger-cargo liners: the 13,200grt, 347-passenger *Cambodge*, *Laos* and *Viet-Nam*, trading regularly between Marseille, the Suez, Bombay and the Far East. Slightly smaller were the 12,700grt sisters *Caledonien* and *Tahitien*, which operated from Marseille across to the Caribbean, Panama and the South Pacific islands (such as French Polynesia and New Hebrides), and finally to Sydney. A quartet of 10,900grt sisters – *Ferdinand de Lesseps*, *Jean Laborde*, *La Bourdonnais* and *Pierre Loti* – sailed between Marseille, the Suez Canal and East African ports. Another firm, Chargeurs Reunis, operated passenger-cargo liners – *Louis Lumière*, *Claude Bernard* and *Lavoisier* – between northern European ports and the east coast of South America. Three other company passenger ships, *General Leclerc*, *Brazza* and *Foucauld*, traded between Bordeaux and French West Africa. Compagnie de Navigation Sud-Atlantique also had interests in South American sailings, operating the combination liners *Charles Tellier* and *Laennec* between northern Europe, Rio and Buenos Aires. The Fabre Line had three liners on the Marseille–West Africa route: *General Mangin*, *Jean Mermoz* and *Foch*. On the same service was the Compagnie de Navigation Paquet with the 10,000grt *Lyuatey*, as well as the *Djenne* and *Koutoubia*. Compagnie de Navigation Mixte looked mostly

Capped by her enormous single funnel, *Pasteur* arrives at Halifax with returning troops in this 1945 view. (Halifax Maritime Museum)

Other French passenger ships: *Cambodge* and her two twin sisters sailed between Marseille and the Far East for Messageries Maritimes. (Author's Collection)

Pierre Loti, also belonging to Messageries Maritimes, sailed between Marseille and East African ports. (Richard Faber Collection)

Paquet Lines' *Djenne* was used in service to West African ports from Marseille. (Gillespie-Faber Collection)

Bretagne and her sister, *Provence*, were important liners on the Mediterranean–east coast of South America service. (Gillespie-Faber Collection)

to the Algerian trade from Marseille with *Kairouan*, *El Djezair*, *El Mansour* and *President de Cazalet*. Marseille-based Transports Maritimes had four small passenger ships serving North Africa: *Sidi-Bel-Abbes*, *Sidi-Ferruch*, *Sidi-Okba* and *Sidi-Mabrouk*, along with two far larger liners, the 16,000grt sisters *Bretagne* and *Provence*, sailing between Naples, Genoa, Marseille, Barcelona and Dakar to the east coast of South America, to Rio de Janeiro, Santos, Montevideo and Buenos Aires. In all, the French had almost fifty deep-sea passenger ships in service in 1960.

El Mansour, belonging to Compagnie de Navigation Mixte, traded between Marseille and North Africa. (Gillespie-Faber Collection)

Foch of the Fabre Line sailed to colonial French West Africa from Bordeaux. (Gillespie-Faber Collection)

The 12,000grt *Lavoisier* of Chargeurs Reunis, a combination passenger-cargo liner, was used in regular service between northern Europe and the east coast of South America. (Gillespie-Faber Collection)

Belonging to Compagnie de Navigation Sud-Atlantique, *Laennec* also traded to Rio, Santos, Montevideo and Buenos Aires from Le Havre and other north European ports. (Author's Collection)

'The French were never that keen on sea travel. Actually, they never liked being too far away from France itself,' added Philippe Brebant. 'Also, by the 1950s & '60s, most of the French passenger ship lines were privately owned but heavily subsidised by the Government, especially to the colonial outposts [Africa, the Indian Ocean, the Pacific and the Caribbean], for passengers, soldiers, cargo & mail. But as decolonisation began in the '60s, the passenger ship links stopped almost immediately, almost overnight in fact.'

9

REPLACEMENT & THE FUTURE: *FRANCE*

'The planning, actual design and then the final plan to build the *France* was a very long, drawn-out affair,' reported Philippe Brebant:

It all began soon after the war ended, in 1949, but moved slowly, often very slowly. The first idea was for two midsized ships. Then it moved to a larger ship and then it moved to an even larger ship. Then it went to a large ship with less power and speed and then to a large ship with great power and higher speed. Then there was the interruption, if you will, of simply rebuilding an existing liner, the *Pasteur*, to further continue transatlantic service. In reality, by the time the final project was accepted and the *France* began construction, she was already too late. Ideally, based on the original 1949 ideas, she should have come into service in 1954 or 1955. This dragged on until 1962, when, among other factors, the airlines had the jets and the future of Atlantic travel had changed. In looking back, the French made a big error in delaying the creation of their new liner …

It is often said and incorrectly reported that President De Gaulle was the 'creator' of the *France*. The idea of a big, new French liner began in 1949 and so well before De Gaulle became president at the beginning of the Fifth Republic in 1958. The ship had been ordered by the previous regime, during the Presidency of Rene Coty in the Fourth Republic. De Gaulle simply grabbed the prestige & seized the excitement of the building of the ship. The *France* had been ordered in 1956, and construction first began a year later in September 1957.

The 66,348grt *France* sailed for ten months of the year on crossings, made an occasional New York–Mediterranean voyage and otherwise did some cruises in deep winter, mostly two-week itineraries from New York to the Caribbean. 'Amidst the excitement, glamour and even the popularity of the *France* in the 1960s, there were those in France who said "prestige was in the air, not on the seas",' said Brebant. 'There are many stories and tales in France of the passengers, French as well as Americans and others, sailing aboard the *France*. One of the more unusual was of the regular passenger who used to mix his caviar in sorbet!'

The giant *France* is ready to be launched in this aerial view dated 11 May 1960. (Cronican-Arroyo Collection)

A preliminary plan for the 1,035ft-long *France*, the world's longest liner. (Author's Collection)

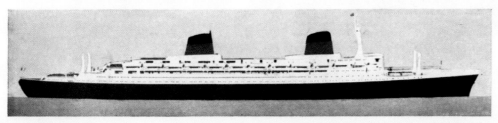

"FRANCE" CARACTÉRISTIQUES COMPARÉES DES PAQUEBOTS "NORMANDIE" ET "FRANCE"

Le paquebot "NORMANDIE", dont la glorieuse renommée a fait le tour du monde, est souvent pris comme base de référence lorsque l'on évoque le futur paquebot "FRANCE". C'est pourquoi nous avons cru bien faire, pour fixer les idées, de rapprocher les caractéristiques principales de ces deux unités. On pourra ainsi mieux constater les différences qui ont été, soit permises par les progrès de la technique, soit imposées par l'évolution de la conjoncture commerciale. "FRANCE" par rapport à "NORMANDIE", est un paquebot :

		"NORMANDIE"	"FRANCE"
— Plus long	. . . .	313 m, 75	315 m, 50
— Plus "fin"	. . . .	36 m, 40 (de large)	33 m, 70
— Plus léger	. . . .	70.000 T.	55.000 T.
— Plus rapide	. . . .	29 nœuds en service	31 nœuds
— Plus économique	. . . .	La consommation sera inférieure de 40 % à celle de "NORMANDIE".	

De plus, si la capacité en passagers du "FRANCE" est légèrement supérieure à celle de "NORMANDIE", la différence réside surtout dans la répartition des classes

Passagers 1re Classe	. . . .	848	500
» Classe Cabine (2e Classe)	. . .	665	—
» Classe Touriste (3e Classe)	. .	458	1.500

COMPAGNIE GÉNÉRALE TRANSATLANTIQUE

PARIS - 6, RUE AUBER - OPE. 02-00 & RIC. 97-59

IMPRIMERIE TRANSATLANTIQUE, PARIS.

France enters the graving dock at Le Havre for the first time in January 1961. *Liberté* is to the right in the far distance, while the all-white *Colombie* is to the right. (Philippe Brebant Collection)

In the end, the 1,035ft-long *France* sailed for only twelve years and then was laid up at Le Havre for another five years, until August 1979. 'There were many reasons that led to the premature and sudden withdrawal of the *France* [in September 1974],' reported Philippe Brebant:

One initial reason had to do with the frequent changing of the crew. Backed by the very powerful French unions, crew members had shorter and shorter periods on the ship. In the end, they were even changing at New York and so replacements had to be flown over from France, returning crew being flown home.

Ironically, the big French seamen's union is called CGT, just like CGT – the Compagnie Generale Transatlantique. The union stood for Compagnie Generale des Travailleurs. They are still around today [2012]. But back in the days of the French liners, they were often creating as well as causing problems – such as last-minute strikes and usually just before sailings from Le Havre. Their basic motto was 'work less for more money' …

Heading off on her maiden crossing to New York, the splendid *France* departs from Le Havre. (Richard Faber Collection)

The increasingly high cost of fuel oil was another major blow to the ship. There were also reports that many top passengers, celebrities as well as French Government officials and 'friends' of the Government, were 'guests' of the French Line, aboard the state-owned *France* …

The final blow was the cut by the Government of subsidies to the *France*. These were absolutely essential, like a blood line, to the ship and her future operation. Of course, there were the high salaries as demanded by the unions. The *France* had a very large crew and the unions would not allow any reductions. Furthermore, they refused to cut or reduce wages. Often, they also had strikes and usually just before sailing, when the passengers were boarding or already on board. More than anything the French unions killed the ship!

Business on the North Atlantic was declining rapidly by the mid-1970s (there were even reduced student fares for those up to the age of 30 to help fill tourist-class berths on board *France*) and as the North American cruise trades were growing, expanding, but also becoming more specialised and competitive. To complicate matters even further, the price of fuel oil had jumped (in 1973) from $35 to $95 per ton. The French Government would have to increase its annual subsidy for the less and less popular *France* from $14 million to $24 million. Instead, Paris ministers voted to support Air France and their new Concorde project.

After being laid up in the backwaters of Le Havre from October 1974, *France* was sold, in 1976, to Arab millionaire Akram Ojjeh for $22 million. His plan was to use her as a combination museum, hotel and casino while moored off Daytona Beach, Florida. The project never materialised and so the ship went back on the sales lists. The Soviets, the Chinese and the Arabs were said to be interested, as well as Club Med and Taiwanese scrap merchants; but instead, in 1979, she was sold to Norwegian Klosters Rederi for their Miami-based Norwegian Caribbean Lines division. She was extensively rebuilt at Bremerhaven, West Germany (at a cost of over $150 million), emerging in May 1980 as the restyled, more tropical *Norway*, carrying up to 2,181 passengers all in one class. She was used mostly on weekly seven-day cruises from Miami to the eastern Caribbean and later on occasional European voyages. She even made several nostalgic voyages aimed at the French, but then had a headline-making explosion at Miami in May 2003. She was promptly retired and laid up (at Bremerhaven) amidst countless rumours of revival, including one which proposed using her for one-night Far Eastern gambling cruises. Nothing came to pass and finally, renamed *Blue Lady*, she was sold to Indian shipbreakers and broken up at Gadani Beach in 2009 after a career lasting forty-seven years.

Silent and lonely, the Chambord Restaurant aboard the laid-up *France* in 1975. (French Line)

Philippe Brebant added:

There is nostalgia in the old French Line and its ships, and for ocean liners. Today [2010], travellers in France increasingly look to cruising, but, with the French Line itself long gone, to voyages on mostly foreign-flag passenger ships. Costa, MSC Cruises and Louis Cruise Lines are the big sellers in the current French cruise market. There is also *Bleu de France/ Horizon* ... But in fact, there is still a connection to the French Line. Its successor, CGM, the Compagnie Generale Maritime, which owns and operates a very large container-cargo company, also owns some 70 per cent of Marseille-based Ponant Cruises. They operate as many as six cruise ships including the 2011-built, 264-passenger sisters *L'Austral* and *Le Boreal* [Ponant Cruises was sold to British buyers in 2012] ...

French tour and travel firms also charter entire ships, such as the Portuguese-owned *Princess Danae*, which carries some French staff and all-French passengers. French vacationers do not like to be 'disconnected' from France itself. They like to have French travellers around them, speak French, eat French foods and of course drink French wines.

Also, but with more excitement and possible anticipation than reality, there is a project aimed at creating a 'new' *France* and even having her sail under the Tricolour. She would be built at St Nazaire and would be 60,000 tons and carry 700 passengers. 'This is a private venture, however, and well away from existing French shipping,' revealed Brebant. 'If such a ship were to come about, there would be major problems with the French unions. This, in the end, makes it all look very doubtful. Instead, we have the great history and legend of the French liners of the past, classic liners such as the *Île de France & Liberté*.'

France being towed away to Bremerhaven, Germany, to become the cruise ship *Norway*, August 1979. (Norwegian Cruise Lines)

BIBLIOGRAPHY

Braynard, Frank O. & Miller, William H., *Fifty Famous Liners*, Vols 1–3 (Cambridge: Patrick Stephens Ltd, 1982–87).

Braynard, Frank O., *Lives of the Liners* (New York: Cornell Maritime Press, 1947).

Dunn, Laurence, *Passenger Liners* (Southampton: Adlard Coles Ltd, 1961).

Haws, Duncan, *Merchants Fleets: French Line* (Uckfield: TCL Productions, 1996).

Kludas, Arnold, *Great Passenger Ships of the World*, Vols 1–5 (Cambridge: Patrick Stephens Ltd, 1972–76).

Mayes, William, *Cruise Ships*, 4th edn (Windsor: Overview Press Ltd, 2011).

Miller, William H., *Pictorial Encyclopaedia of Ocean Liners 1860–1994* (New York: Dover Publications Inc., 1995).

———, *Picture History of the French Line* (New York: Dover Publications Inc., 1997).

Official Steamship Guide (New York: Transportation Guides Inc., 1937–63).

Olivier, Frederic, Perrov, Aymeric & Senant, Frank, *A Bord des Paquebots* (Paris: Norma Editions, 2011).